Notes Of Class Talks And Lectures -II

by

Swami Vivekananda

Double 9 BOOKS

Notes Of Class Talks And Lectures –II

by Swami Vivekananda

ISBN: 978-93-59393-72-8

Published by

DOUBLE 9 BOOKS

2/13-B, Ansari Road
Daryaganj, New Delhi – 110002
info@double9books.com
www.double9books.com
Tel. 011-40042856

ABOUT THE AUTHOR

Swami Vivekananda was born Narendranath Datta in India on January 12, 1863. He died on July 4, 1902, and was the most important student of the Indian saint Ramakrishna. He was an important part of bringing Vedanta and Yoga to the West. He is also charged with making people more aware of other religions and making Hinduism a major world religion. Vivekananda had a lot of success at the Parliament. In the years that followed, he gave hundreds of lectures across the United States, England, and Europe to spread the main ideas of Hinduism. He also started the Vedanta Society of New York and the Vedanta Society of San Francisco, which is now the Vedanta Society of Northern California. Both of these groups became the basis for Vedanta Societies in the West. Vivekananda was one of the most important philosophers and social reformers in India at the time. He was also one of the most successful and powerful Vedanta missionaries in the West.People now think of him as one of the most important people in modern India and Hinduism. Mahatma Gandhi said that after reading Vivekananda's works, he loved his country a thousand times more.

CONTENTS

Religion And Science 7

Religion Is Realisation 9

Religion Is Self-Abnegation 10

Unselfish Work Is True Renunciation 11

Freedom Of The Self 12

Notes On Vedanta 13

Hindu And Greek 14

Thoughts On The Vedas And The Upanishads 15

On Raja-Yoga 17

On Bhakti-Yoga 18

On Jnana-Yoga 20

The Reality And Shadow 21

How To Become Free 22

Soul And God 23

The Goal 24

On Proof Of Religion 25

The Design Theory 27

Spirit And Nature 29

The Practice Of Religion 31

Fragmentary Notes On The Ramayana 32

Notes Taken Down In Madras, 1892-93 33

Concentration 49

The Power Of The Mind 51

Lessons On Raja-Yoga 53

Lessons On Bhakti-Yoga 60

Mother-Worship 67

Narada-Bhakti-Sutras 71

Religion And Science

Experience is the only source of knowledge. In the world, religion is the only science where there is no surety, because it is not taught as a science of experience. This should not be. There is always, however, a small group of men who teach religion from experience. They are called mystics, and these mystics in every religion speak the same tongue and teach the same truth. This is the real science of religion. As mathematics in every part of the world does not differ, so the mystics do not differ. They are all similarly constituted and similarly situated. Their experience is the same; and this becomes law.

In the church, religionists first learn a religion, then begin to practice it; they do not take experience as the basis of their belief. But the mystic starts out in search of truth, experiences it first, and then formulates his creed. The church takes the experience of others; the mystic has his own experience. The church goes from the outside in; the mystic goes from the inside out.

Religion deals with the truths of the metaphysical world just as chemistry and the other natural sciences deal with the truths of the physical world. The book one must read to learn chemistry is the book of nature. The book from which to learn religion is your own mind and heart. The sage is often ignorant of physical science, because he reads the wrong book — the book within; and the scientist is too often ignorant of religion, because he too reads the wrong book — the book without.

All science has its particular methods; so has the science of religion. It has more methods also, because it has more material to work upon. The human mind is not homogeneous like the external world. According to the different nature, there must be different methods. As some special sense predominates in a person — one person will see most, another will hear most — so there is a predominant mental sense; and through this gate must each reach his own mind. Yet through all minds runs a unity, and there is a science which may be applied to all. This science of religion is based on the analysis of the human soul. It has no creed.

No one form of religion will do for all. Each is a pearl on a string. We must be particular above all else to find individuality in each. No man is born to any religion; he has a religion in his own soul. Any system which seeks to destroy individuality is in the long run disastrous. Each life has a current running through it, and this current will eventually take it to God. The end and aim of all religions is to realise God. The greatest of all training is to worship God alone. If each man chose his own ideal and stuck to it, all religious controversy would vanish.

Religion Is Realisation

The greatest name man ever gave to God is Truth. Truth is the fruit of realisation; therefore seek it within the soul. Get away from all books and forms and let your soul see its Self. "We are deluded and maddened by books", Shri Krishna declares. Be beyond the dualities of nature. The moment you think creed and form and ceremony the "be-all" and "end-all", then you are in bondage. Take part in them to help others, but take care they do not become a bondage. Religion is one, but its application must be various. Let each one, therefore, give his message; but find not the defects in other religions. You must come out from all form if you would see the Light. Drink deep of the nectar of the knowledge of God. The man who realises. "I am He", though clad in rags, is happy. Go forth into the Eternal and come back with eternal energy. The slave goes out to search for truth; he comes back free.

Religion Is Self-Abnegation

One cannot divide the rights of the universe. To talk of "right" implies limitation. It is not "right" but "responsibility". Each is responsible for the evil anywhere in the world. No one can separate himself from his brother. All that unites with the universal is virtue; all that separates is sin. You are a part of the Infinite. This is your nature. Hence you are your brother's keeper.

The first end of life is knowledge; the second end of life is happiness. Knowledge and happiness lead to freedom. But not one can attain liberty until every being (ant or dog) has liberty. Not one can be happy until all are happy. When you hurt anyone you hurt yourself, for you and your brother are one. He is indeed a Yogi who sees himself in the whole universe and the whole universe in himself. Self-sacrifice, not self-assertion, is the law of the highest universe. The world is so evil because Jesus' teaching, "Resist not evil", has never been tried. Selflessness alone will solve the problem. Religion comes with intense self-sacrifice. Desire nothing for yourself. Do all for others. This is to live and move and have your being in God.

Unselfish Work Is True Renunciation

This world is not for cowards. Do not try to fly. Look not for success or failure. Join yourself to the perfectly unselfish will and work on. Know that the mind which is born to succeed joins itself to a determined will and perseveres. You have the right to work, but do not become so degenerate as to look for results. Work incessantly, but see something behind the work. Even good deeds can find a man in great bondage. Therefore be not bound by good deeds or by desire for name and fame. Those who know this secret pass beyond this round of birth and death and become immortal.

The ordinary Sannyâsin gives up the world, goes out, and thinks of God. The real Sannyâsin lives in the world, but is not of it. Those who deny themselves, live in the forest, and chew the cud of unsatisfied desires are not true renouncers. Live in the midst of the battle of life. Anyone can keep calm in a cave or when asleep. Stand in the whirl and madness of action and reach the Centre. If you have found the Centre, you cannot be moved.

Freedom Of The Self

As we cannot know except through effects that we have eyes, so we cannot see the Self except by Its effects. It cannot be brought down to the low plane of sense-perception. It is the condition of everything in the universe, though Itself unconditioned. When we know that we are the Self, then we are free. The Self can never change. It cannot be acted on by a cause, because It is Itself the cause. It is self-caused. If we can find in ourself something that is not acted on by any cause, then we have known the Self.

Freedom is inseparably connected with immortality. To be free one must be above the laws of nature. Law exists so long as we are ignorant. When knowledge comes, then we find that law nothing but freedom in ourselves. The will can never be free, because it is the slave of cause and effect. But the "I" behind the will is free; and this is the Self. "I am free" — that is the basis on which to build and live. And freedom means immortality.

Notes On Vedanta

The cardinal features of the Hindu religion are founded on the meditative and speculative philosophy and on the ethical teachings contained in the various books of the Vedas, which assert that the universe is infinite in space and eternal in duration. It never had a beginning and it never will have an end. Innumerable have been the manifestations of the power of the Spirit in the realm of matter, of the force or the Infinite in the domain of the finite, but the Infinite Itself is self-existent, eternal, and unchangeable. The passage of time makes no mark whatever on the dial of eternity. In its super Sensuous region, which cannot be comprehended at all by the human understanding, there is no past and there is no future.

The Vedas teach that the soul of man is immortal. The body is subject to the law of growth and decay what grows must of necessity decay. But the indwelling spirit is related to the infinite and eternal life; it never had a beginning, and it will never have an end. One of the chief distinctions between the Vedic and the Christian religion is that the Christian religion teaches that each human soul had its beginning at its birth into this world; whereas the Vedic religion asserts that the spirit of man is an emanation of the Eternal Being and had no more a beginning than God Himself. Innumerable have been and will be its manifestations in its passage from one personality to another, subject to the great law of spiritual evolution, until it reaches perfection, when there is no more change.

Hindu And Greek

Three mountains stand as typical of progress — the Himalayas of Indo-Aryan, Sinai of Hebrew, and Olympus of Greek civilisation. When the Aryans reached India, they found the climate so hot that they would not work incessantly, so they began to think; thus they became introspective and developed religion. They discovered that there was no limit to the power of mind; they therefore sought to master that; and through it they learnt that there was something infinite coiled up in the frame we call man, which was seeking to become kinetic. To evolve this became their chief aim. Another branch of the Aryans went into the smaller and more picturesque country of Greece, where the climate and natural conditions were more favourable; so their activity turned outwards, and they developed the external arts and outward liberty. The Greek sought political liberty. The Hindu has always sought spiritual liberty. Both are one-sided. The Indian cares not enough for national protection or patriotism, he will defend only his religion; while with the Greek and in Europe (where the Greek civilisation finds its continuation) the country comes first. To care only for spiritual liberty and not for social liberty is a defect, but the opposite is a still greater defect. Liberty of both soul and body is to be striven for.

Thoughts On The Vedas And The Upanishads

The Vedic sacrificial altar was the origin of Geometry.

The invocation of the Devas, or bright ones, was the basis of worship. The idea is that one invoked is helped and helps.

Hymns are not only words of praise but words of power, being pronounced with the right attitude of mind.

Heavens are only other states of existence with added senses and heightened powers.

All higher bodies also are subject to disintegration as is the physical. Death comes to all forms of bodies in this and other lives. Devas are also mortal and can only give enjoyment.

Behind all Devas there is the Unit Being — God, as behind this body there is something higher that feels and sees.

The powers of creation, preservation, and destruction of the Universe, and the attributes, such as omnipresence, omniscience, and omnipotence, make God of gods.

"Hear ye children of Immortality! Hear ye Devas who live in higher spheres!" (Shvetâshvatara, II. 5). "I have found out a ray beyond all darkness, beyond all doubt. I have found the Ancient One" (*ibid*. III. 8). The way to this is contained in the Upanishads.

On earth we die. In heaven we die. In the highest heaven we die. It is only when we reach God that we attain life and become immortal.

The Upanishads treat of this alone. The path of the Upanishads is the pure path. Many manners, customs, and local allusions cannot be understood today. Through them, however, truth becomes clear. Heavens and Earth are all thrown off in order to come to Light.

The Upanishads declare:

"He the Lord has interpenetrated the universe. It is all His."

"He the Omnipresent, the One without a second, the One without a body, pure, the great poet of the universe, whose metre is the suns and stars, is giving to each what he deserves" (Isha Upanishad, 8, adapted).

"They are groping in utter darkness who try to reach the Light by ceremonials. And they who think this nature is all are in darkness. They who wish to come out of nature through this thought are groping in still deeper darkness" (Isha, 9).

Are then ceremonials bad? No, they will benefit those who are coming on.

In one of the Upanishads (i.e. Katha) this question is asked by Nachiketâ, a youth: "Some say of a dead man, he is gone; others, he is still living. You are Yama, Death. You know the truth; do answer me." Yama replies, "Even the Devas, many of them, know not — much less men. Boy, do not ask of me this answer." But Nachiketa persists. Yama again replies, "The enjoyments of the gods, even these I offer you. Do not insist upon your query." But Nachiketa was firm as a rock. Then the god of death said, "My boy, you have declined, for the third time, wealth, power, long life, fame, family. You are brave enough to ask the highest truth. I will teach you. There are two ways, one of truth; one of enjoyment. You have chosen the former."

Now note here the conditions of imparting the truth. First, the purity — a boy, a pure, unclouded soul, asking the secret of the universe. Second, that he must take truth for truth's sake alone.

Until the truth has come through one who has had realisation, from one who has perceived it himself, it cannot become fruitful. Books cannot give it, argument cannot establish it. Truth comes unto him who knows the secret of it.

After you have received it, be quiet. Be not ruffled by vain argument. Come to your own realization. You alone can do it.

Neither happiness nor misery, vice nor virtue, knowledge nor non-knowledge is it. You must realise it. How can I describe it to you?

He who cries out with his whole heart, "O Lord, I want but Thee" — to him the Lord reveals Himself. Be pure, be calm; the mind when ruffled cannot reflect the Lord.

"He whom the Vedas declare, He, to reach whom, we serve with prayer and sacrifice, Om is the sacred name of that indescribable One. This word is the holiest of all words. He who knows the secret of this word receives that which he desires." Take refuge in this word. Whoso takes refuge in this word, to him the way opens.

On Raja-Yoga

The first stage of Yoga is Yama.

To master Yama five things are necessary:

(1) Non-injuring any being by thought, word, and deed.

(2) Speaking the truth in thought, word, and deed

(3) Non-covetousness in thought, word, and deed.

(4) Perfect chastity in thought, word, and deed.

(5) Perfect sinlessness in thought, word, and deed.

Holiness is the greatest power. Everything else quails before it.

Then come Âsana, or posture, of a devotee. The seat must be firm, the head, ribs, and body in a straight line, erect. Say to yourself that you are firmly seated, and that nothing can move you. Then mention the perfection of the body, bit by bit, from head to foot. Think of it as being dear as crystal, and as a perfect vessel to sail over the sea of life.

Pray to God and to all the prophets and saviours of the world and holy spirits in the universe to help you.

Then for half an hour practice Prânâyama or the suspending, restraining, and controlling of the breath, mentally repeating the word Om as you inhale and exhale the breath. Words charged with spirit have wonderful power.

The other stages of Yoga are: (1) Pratyâhâra or the restraint of the organs of sense from all outward things, and directing them entirely to mental impressions; (2) Dhâranâ or steadfast concentration; (3) Dhyâna or meditation; (4) Samâdhi or abstract meditation. It is the highest and last stage of Yoga. Samadhi is perfect absorption of thought into the Supreme Spirit, when one realises. "I and my Father are one."

Do one thing at a time and while doing it put your whole soul into it to the exclusion of all else.

On Bhakti-Yoga

Bhakti-Yoga is the path of systematised devotion for the attainment of union with the Absolute. It is the easiest and surest path to religion or realisation.

Love to God is the one essential to be perfect in this path.

There are five stages of love.

First, man wants help and has a little fear.

Second, when God is seen as Father.

Third, when God is seen as Mother. Then all women are looked upon as reflections of the Mother-God. With the idea of Mother-God real love begins.

Fourth, love for love's sake. Love for love's sake transcends all qualities.

Fifth, love in Divine-union. It leads to oneness or superconsciousness.

God is both Personal and Impersonal as we are personal and impersonal.

Prayer and praise are the first means of growth. Repeating the names of God has wonderful power.

Mantra is a special word, or sacred text, or name of God chosen by the Guru for repetition and reflection by the disciple. The disciple must concentrate on a personality for prayer and praise, and that is his Ishta.

These words (Mantras) are not sounds of words but God Himself, and we have them within us. Think of Him, speak of Him. No desire for the world! Buddha's Sermon on the Mount was, "As thou thinkest, so art thou."

After attaining superconsciousness the Bhakta descends again to love and worship.

Pure love has no motive. It has nothing to gain.

After prayer and praise comes meditation. Then comes reflection on the name and on the Ishta of the individual.

Pray that that manifestation which is our Father, our Mother, may cut our bonds.

Pray, "Take us by the hand as a father takes his sons and leave us not."

Pray, "I do not want wealth or beauty, this world or another, but Thee, O God! Lord! I have become weary. Oh, take me by the hand, Lord, I take shelter with Thee Make me Thy servant. Be Thou my refuge."

Pray, "Thou our Father, our Mother, our dearest Friend! Thou who bearest this universe, help us to bear the little burden of this our life. Leave us not. Let us never be separated from Thee. Let us always dwell in Thee."

When love to God is revealed and is all, this world appears like a drop.

Pass from non-existence to existence, from darkness to light.

On Jnana-Yoga

First, meditation should be of a negative nature. Think away everything. Analyse everything that comes in the mind by the sheer action of the will.

Next, assert what we really are — existence, knowledge and bliss — being, knowing, and loving.

Meditation is the means of unification of the subject and object. Meditate:

Above, it is full of me; below, it is full of me; in the middle, it is full of me. I am in all beings, and all beings are in me. Om Tat Sat, I am It. I am existence above mind. I am the one Spirit of the universe. I am neither pleasure nor pain.

The body drinks, eats, and so on. I am not the body. I am not mind. I am He.

I am the witness. I look on. When health comes I am the witness When disease comes I am the witness.

I am Existence, Knowledge, Bliss.

I am the essence and nectar of knowledge. Through eternity I change not. I am calm, resplendent, and unchanging.

The Reality And Shadow

That which differentiates one thing from another is time, space, and causation.

The differentiation is in the form, not in the substance.

You may destroy the form and it disappears for ever; but the substance remains the same. You can never destroy the substance.

Evolution is in nature, not in the soul — evolution of nature, manifestation of the soul.

Maya is not illusion as it is popularly interpreted. Maya is real, yet it is not real. It is real in that the Real is behind it and gives it its appearance of reality. That which is real in Maya is the Reality in and through Maya. Yet the Reality is never seen; and hence that which is seen is unreal, and its has no real independent existence of itself, but is dependent upon the Real for its existence.

Maya then is a paradox — real, yet not real, an illusion, yet not an illusion.

He who knows the Real sees in Maya not illusion, but reality. He who knows not the Real sees in Maya illusion and thinks it real.

How To Become Free

All things in nature work according to law. Nothing is excepted. The mind as well as everything in external nature is governed and controlled by law.

Internal and external nature, mind and matter, are in time and space, and are bound by the law of causation.

The freedom of the mind is a delusion. How can the mind be free when it is controlled and bound by law?

The law of Karma is the law of causation.

We must become free. We are free; the work is to know it. We must give up all slavery, all bondage of whatever kind. We must not only give up our bondage to earth and everything and everybody on earth, but also to all ideas of heaven and happiness.

We are bound to earth by desire and also to God, heaven, and the angels. A slave is a slave whether to man, to God, or to angels.

The idea of heaven must pass away. The idea of heaven after death where the good live a life of eternal happiness is a vain dream, without a particle of meaning or sense in it. Wherever there is happiness there must follow unhappiness sometime. Wherever there is pleasure there must be pain. This is absolutely certain, every action has its reaction somehow.

The idea of freedom is the only true idea of salvation — freedom from everything, the senses, whether of pleasure or pain, from good as well as evil.

More than this even, we must be free from death and to be free from death, we must be free from life. Life is but a dream of death. Where there is life, there will be death; so get away from life if you would be rid of death.

We are ever free if we would only believe it, only have faith enough. You are the soul, free and eternal, ever free ever blessed. Have faith enough and you will be free in a minute.

Everything in time, space, and causation is bound. The soul is beyond all time, all space, all causation. That which is bound is nature, not the soul.

Therefore proclaim your freedom and be what you are — ever free, ever blessed.

Time, space, and causation we call Maya.

Soul And God

Anything that is in space has form. Space itself has form. Either you are in space, or space is in you. The soul is beyond all space. Space is in the soul, not the soul in space.

Form is confined to time and space and is bound by the law of causation. All time is in us, we are not in time. As the soul is not in time and space, all time and space are within the soul. The soul is therefore omnipresent.

Our idea of God is the reflection of ourselves.

Old Persian and Sanskrit have affinities.

The primitive idea of God was identifying God with different forms of nature — nature-worship. The next stage was the tribal God. The next stage, the worship of kings.

The idea of God in heaven is predominant in all nations except in India. The idea is very crude.

The idea of the continuity of life is foolish. We can never get rid of death until we get rid of life.

The Goal

Dualism recognises God and nature to be eternally separate: the universe and nature eternally dependent upon God.

The extreme monists make no such distinction. In the last analysis, they claim, all is God: the universe becomes lost in God; God is the eternal life of the universe.

With them infinite and finite are mere terms. The universe, nature, etc. exist by virtue of differentiation. Nature is itself differentiation.

Such questions as, "Why did God create the universe?" "Why did the All-perfect create the imperfect?" etc., can never be answered, because such questions are logical absurdities. Reason exists in nature; beyond nature it has no existence. God is omnipotent, hence to ask why He did so and so is to limit Him; for it implies that there is a purpose in His creating the universe. If He has a purpose, it must be a means to an end, and this would mean that He could not have the end without the means. The questions, why and wherefore, can only be asked of something which depends upon something else.

On Proof Of Religion

The great question about religion is: What makes it so unscientific? If religion is a science, why is it not as certain as other sciences? All beliefs in God, heaven, etc., are mere conjectures, mere beliefs. There seems to be nothing certain about it. Our ideas concerning religion are changing all the time. The mind is in a constant state of flux.

Is man a soul, an unchanging substance, or is he a constantly changing quantity? All religions, except primitive Buddhism, believe that man is a soul, an identity, a unit that never dies but is immortal.

The primitive Buddhists believe that man is a constantly changing quantity, and that his consciousness consists in an almost infinite succession of incalculably rapid changes, each change, as it were, being unconnected with the others, standing alone, thus precluding the theory of the law of sequence or causation.

If there is a unit, there is a substance. A unit is always simple. A simple is not a compound of anything. It does not depend on anything else. It stands alone and is immortal.

Primitive Buddhists contend that everything is unconnected; nothing is a unit; and that the theory of man being a unit is a mere belief and cannot be proved.

Now the great question is: Is man a unit, or is he a constantly changing mass?

There is but one way to prove this, to answer this question. Stop the gyrations of the mind, and the theory that a man is a unit, a simple, will be demonstrated. All changes are in me, in the Chitta, the mind-substance. I am not the changes. If I were, I could not stop them.

Everyone is trying to make himself and everybody else believe that this world is all very fine, that he is perfectly happy. But when man stops to question his motives in life, he will see that the reason he is struggling after this and that is because he cannot help himself. He must move on. He cannot stop, so he tries to make himself believe that he really wants this and that. The one who actually succeeds in making himself believe that he is having a good time is the man of splendid physical health. This man responds to his desires instantly, without question. He acts in response to that power within him, urging him on without a thought, as though he acted because he wanted to. But when he has been knocked about a good deal by nature, when he has received a good many wounds and bruises, he begins to question the meaning of all this; and as he gets hurt more and thinks more, he sees that he is urged on by a power beyond his control and that he acts simply because he must. Then he begins to rebel, and the battle begins.

Now if there is a way out of all this trouble, it is within ourselves. We are always trying to realise the Reality. Instinctively we are always trying to do that. It is creation in the human soul that covers up God; that is why there is so much difference in God-ideals. Only when creation stops can we find the Absolute. The Absolute is in the soul, not in creation. So by stopping creation, we come to know the Absolute. When we think of ourselves, we think of the body; and when we think of God, we think of Him as body. To stop the gyrations of the mind, so that the soul may become manifested, is the work. Training begins with the body. Breathing trains the body, gets it into a harmonious condition. The object of the breathing exercises is to attain meditation and concentration. If you can get absolutely still for just one moment, you have reached the goal. The mind may go on working after that; but it will never be the same mind again. You will know yourself as you are — your true Self. Still the mind but for one moment, and the truth of your real nature will flash upon you, and freedom is at hand: no more bondage after that. This follows from the theory that if you can know an instant of time, you know all time, as the whole is the rapid succession of one. Master the one know thoroughly one instant — and freedom is reached.

All religions believe in God and the soul except the primitive Buddhist. The modern Buddhists believe in God and the soul. Among the primitive Buddhists are the Burmese, Siamese, Chinese, etc.

Arnold's book, *The Light of Asia*, represents more of Vedantism than Buddhism.

The Design Theory

The idea that nature in all her orderly arrangements shows design on the part of the Creator of the universe is good as a kindergarten teaching to show the beauty, power, and glory of God, in order to lead children in religion up to a philosophical conception of God; but apart from that, it is not good, and perfectly illogical. As a philosophical idea, it is entirely without foundation, if God is taken to be omnipotent.

If nature shows the power of God in creating the universe, (then) to have a design in so doing also shows His weakness. If God is omnipotent, He needs no design, no scheme, to do anything. He has but to will it, and it is done. No question, no scheme, no plan, of God in nature.

The material universe is the result of the limited consciousness of man. When man becomes conscious of his divinity, all matter, all nature, *as we know it*, will cease to exist.

The material world, as such, has no place in the consciousness of the All-Presence as a necessity of any end. If it had, God would be limited by the universe. To say that nature exists by His permission is not to say that it exists as a necessity for Him to make man perfect, or for any other reason.

It is a creation for man's necessity, not God's. There, is no scheme of God in the plan of the universe. How could there be any if He is omnipotent? Why should He have need of a plan, or a scheme, or a reason to do anything? To say that He has is to limit Him and to rob Him of His character of omnipotence.

For instance, if you came to a very wide river, so wide that you could not get across it except by building a bridge, the very fact that you would have to build the bridge to get across the river would show your limitation, would show your weakness, even if the ability to build the bridge did show your strength. If you were not limited but could just fly or jump across, you would not be under the necessity of building the bridge; and to build the bridge just to exhibit your power to do so would show your weakness again by showing your vanity, more than it would show anything else.

Monism and dualism are essentially the same. The difference consists in the expression. As the dualists hold the Father and Son to be two, the monists hold them to be really one. Dualism is in nature, in manifestation, and monism is pure spirituality in the essence.

The idea of renunciation and sacrifice is in all religions as a means to reach God.

Spirit And Nature

Religion is the realisation of Spirit as Spirit; not Spirit as matter.

Religion is a growth. Each one must experience it himself. The Christians believe that Jesus Christ died to save man. With you it is belief in a doctrine, and this belief constitutes your salvation. With us doctrine has nothing whatever to do with salvation. Each one may believe in whatever doctrine he likes; or in no doctrine. What difference does it make to you whether Jesus Christ lived at a certain time or not? What has it to do with you that Moses saw God in the burning bush? The fact that Moses saw God in the burning bush does not constitute your seeing Him, does it? If it does, then the fact that Moses ate is enough for you; you ought to stop eating. One is just as sensible as the other. Records of great spiritual men of the past do us no good whatever except that they urge us onward to do the same, to experience religion ourselves. Whatever Christ or Moses or anybody else did does not help us in the least, except to urge us on.

Each one has a special nature peculiar to himself which he must follow and through which he will find his way to freedom. Your teacher should be able to tell you what your particular path in nature is and to put you in it. He should know by your face where you belong and should be able to indicate it to you. You should never try to follow another's path, for that is his way, not yours. When that path is found, you have nothing to do but fold your arms, and the tide will carry you to freedom. Therefore when you find it, never swerve from it. Your way is the best for you, but that is no sign that it is the best for others.

The truly spiritual see Spirit as Spirit, not as matter. It is Spirit that makes nature move; It is the reality in nature. So action is in nature; not in the Spirit. Spirit is always the same, changeless, eternal. Spirit and matter are in reality the same; but Spirit, as such, never becomes matter; and matter, as such, never becomes Spirit.

The Spirit never acts. Why should it? It merely is, and that is sufficient. It is pure existence absolute and has no need of action.

You are not bound by law. That is in your nature. The mind is in nature and is bound by law. All nature is bound by law, the law of its own action;

and this law can never be broken. If you could break a law of nature, all nature would come to an end in an instant. There would be no more nature. He who attains freedom breaks the law of nature, and for him nature fades away and has no more power over him. Each one will break the law but once and for ever; and that will end his trouble with nature.

Governments, societies, etc. are comparative evils. All societies are based on bad generalization. The moment you form yourselves into an organization, you begin to hate everybody outside of that organization. When you join an organisation, you are putting bounds upon yourself, you are limiting your own freedom. The greatest goodness is the highest freedom. Our aim should be to allow the individual to move towards this freedom. More of goodness, less of artificial laws. Such laws are not laws at all. If it were a law, it could not be broken. The fact that these so-called laws are broken, shows clearly that they are not laws. A law is that which cannot be broken.

Whenever you suppress a thought, it is simply pressed down out of sight, in a coil like a spring, only to spring out again at a moment's notice, with all the pent-up force resulting from the suppression, and do in a few moments what it would have done in a much longer period.

Every ounce of pleasure brings its pound of pain. It is the same energy that at one time manifests itself as pleasure, at another time as pain. As soon as one set of sensations stops, another begins. But in some cases, in more advanced persons, one may have two, yea, even a hundred different thoughts entering into active operation at the same time.

Mind is action of its own nature. Mind-activity means creation. The thought is followed by the word, and the word by the form. All of this creating will have to stop, both mental and physical, before the mind can reflect the soul.

The Practice Of Religion

(At Alameda, Calif., March 18, 1900)

We read many books, but that does not bring us knowledge. We may read all the Bibles in the world, but that will not give us religion. Theoretical religion is easy enough to get, any one may get that. What we want is practical religion.

The Christian idea of a practical religion is in doing good works — worldly utility.

What good is utility? Judged from a utilitarian standpoint, religion is a failure. Every hospital is a prayer that more people may come there. What is meant by charity? Charity is not fundamental. It is really helping on the misery of the world, not eradicating it. One looks for name and fame and covers his efforts to obtain them with the enamel of charity and good works. He is working for himself under the pretext of working for others. Every so-called charity is an encouragement of the very evil it claims to operate against.

Men and women go to balls and dance all night in honour of some hospital or other charitable institution then go home, behave like beasts, and bring devils into the world to fill jails, insane asylums, and hospitals. So it goes on, and it is called good works — building hospital etc. The ideal of good works is to lessen, or eradicate, the misery of the world. The Yogi says, all misery comes from not being able to control the mind. The Yogi's ideal is freedom from nature. Conquest of nature is his standard of work. The Yogi says that all power is in the soul, and by the controlling of the mind and body one conquers nature by the power of the soul.

Every ounce of muscle in excess of what is beyond the needs of one's physical work is that much less of brain. Do not exercise too hard; it is injurious. The one who does not work hard will live the longest. Eat less food and work less. Store up brain food.

Household work is enough for women.

Do not make the lamp burn fast; let it burn slowly.

Proper diet means simple diet, not highly spiced.

Fragmentary Notes On The Ramayana

Worship Him who alone stands by us, whether we are doing good or are doing evil; who never leaves us even; as love never pulls down, as love knows no barter, no selfishness.

Râma was the soul of the old king; but he was a king, and he could not go back on his word.

"Wherever Rama goes, there go I", says Lakshmana, the younger brother

The wife of the elder brother to us Hindus is just like a mother.

At last he found Sitâ, pale and thin, like a bit of the moon that lies low at the foot of the horizon.

Sita was chastity itself; she would never touch the body of another man except that of her husband.

"Pure? She is chastity itself", says Rama.

Drama and music are by themselves religion; any song, love song or any song, never mind; if one's whole soul is in that song, he attains salvation, just by that; nothing else he has to do; if a man's whole soul is in that, his soul gets salvation. They say it leads to the same goal.

Wife — the co-religionist. Hundreds of ceremonies the Hindu has to perform, and not one can be performed if he has not a wife. You see the priests tie them up together, and they go round temples and make very great pilgrimages tied together.

Rama gave up his body and joined Sita in the other world.

Sita — the pure, the pure, the all-suffering!

Sita is the name in India for everything that is goods pure, and holy; everything that in women we call woman.

Sita — the patient, all-suffering, ever-faithful, ever-pure wife! Through all the suffering she had, there was not one harsh word against Rama.

Sita never returned injury.

"Be Sita!"

Notes Taken Down In Madras, 1892-93

The three essentials of Hinduism are belief in God, in the Vedas as revelation, in the doctrine of Karma and transmigration.

If one studies the Vedas between the lines, one sees a religion of harmony.

One point of difference between Hinduism and other religions is that in Hinduism we pass from truth to truth — from a lower truth to a higher truth — and never from error to truth.

The Vedas should be studied through the eye-glass of evolution. They contain the whole history of the progress of religious consciousness, until religion has reached perfection in unity.

The Vedas are Anâdi, eternal. The meaning of the statement is not, as is erroneously supposed by some, that the words of the Vedas are Anadi, but that the spiritual laws inculcated by the Vedas are such. These laws which are immutable and eternal have been discovered at various times by great men or Rishis, though some of them are forgotten now, while others are preserved.

When a number of people from various angles and distances have a look at the sea, each man sees a portion of it according to his horizon. Though each man may say that what he sees is the real sea, all of them speak the truth, for all of them see portions of the same wide expanse. So the religious scriptures, though they seem to contain varying and conflicting statements, speak the truth, for they are all descriptions of that one infinite Reality.

When one sees a mirage for the first time, he mistakes it for a reality, and after vainly trying to quench his thirst in it, learns that it is a mirage. But whenever he sees such a phenomenon in future, in spite of the apparent reality, the idea that he sees a mirage always presents itself to him. So is the world of Mâyâ to a Jivanmukta (the liberated in life).

Some of the Vedic secrets were known to certain families only, as certain powers naturally exist in some families. With the extinction of these families, those secrets have died away.

Vedic anatomy was no less perfect than the Âyurvedic.

There were many names for many parts of the organs, because they had to cut up animals for sacrifice. The sea is described as full of ships. Sea voyage was prohibited later on, partly because there came the fear that people might thereby become Buddhists.

Buddhism was the rebellion of newly-formed Kshatriyas against Vedic priestcraft.

Hinduism threw away Buddhism after taking its sap. The attempt of all the Southern Âchâryas was to effect a reconciliation between the two. Shankarâchârya's teaching shows the influence of Buddhism. His disciples perverted his teaching and carried it to such an extreme point that some of the later reformers were right in calling the Acharya's followers "crypto-Buddhists".

* * *

What is Spencer's unknowable? It is our Maya. Western philosophers are afraid of the unknowable, but our philosophers have taken a big jump into the unknown, and they have conquered.

Western philosophers are like vultures soaring high in the sky, but all the while, with their eye fixed on the carrion beneath. They cannot cross the unknown, and they therefore turn back and worship the almighty dollar.

There have been two lines of progress in this world — political and religious. In the former the Greeks are everything, the modern political institutions being only the development of the Grecian; in the latter the Hindus are everything.

My religion is one of which Christianity is an offshoot and Buddhism a rebel child.

Chemistry ceases to improve when one element is found from which all others are deducible. Physics ceases to progress when one force is found of which all others are manifestations. So religion ceases to progress when unity is reached, which is the case with Hinduism.

There is no new religious idea preached anywhere which is not found in the Vedas.

In everything, there are two kinds of development — analytical and synthetical. In the former the Hindus excel other nations. In the latter they are nil. (Here by the term "synthesis" is meant a scientific generalisation and by the term "analysis" an ontological reduction of facts and objects to their immanent principles. — Ed.)

The Hindus have cultivated the power of analysis and abstraction. No nation has yet produced a grammar like that of Pânini.

Râmânuja's important work is the conversion of Jains and Buddhists to Hinduism. He is a great advocate of image worship. He introduced love and faith as potent means of salvation.

Even in the *Bhâgavata,* twenty-four Avatâras are mentioned corresponding to the twenty-four Tirthankaras of the Jains, the name of Rishibhadeva being common to both.

The practice of Yoga gives the power of abstraction. The superiority of a Siddha over others consists in his being able to separate attributes from objects and think of them independently, giving them objective reality.

* * *

The opposite extremes always meet and resemble each other. The greatest self-forgotten devotee whose mind is absorbed in the contemplation of the infinite Brahman and the most debased, drunken maniac present the same externals. At times we are surprised with the analogical transition from one to the other.

Extremely nervous men succeed as religious men. They become fervent over whatever they take into their head.

"All are mad in this world; some are mad after gold, others after women, and some are after God; if drowning is to be the fate of man, it is better to be drowned in an ocean of milk than in a pool of dung", a devotee replied who was charged with madness.

The God of Infinite Love and the object of Love sublime and infinite are painted blue. Krishna is painted blue, so also Solomon's (See Old Testament, The Song of Solomon, I. 5, 7, 14.) God of Love. It is a natural law that anything sublime and infinite is associated with blue colour. Take a handful of water, it is absolutely colourless. But look at the deep wide ocean; it is as blue as anything. Examine the space near you; it is colourless. But look at the infinite expanse of the sky; it is blue.

That the Hindus, absorbed in the ideal, lacked in realistic observation is evident from this. Take painting and sculpture. What do you see in the Hindu paintings? All sorts of grotesque and unnatural figures. What do you see in a Hindu temple? A Chaturbhanga (Lit. bent at four places or joints of the body.) Nârâyana or some such thing. But take into consideration any Italian picture or Grecian statue — what a study of nature you find in them! A gentleman for twenty years sat burning a candle in his hand, in order to paint a lady carrying a candle in her hand.

The Hindus progressed in the subjective sciences.

There are as many different conducts taught in the Vedas as there are differences in human nature. What is taught to an adult cannot be taught to a child.

A Guru should be a doctor of men. He should understand the nature of his disciple and teach him the method which suits him best.

There are infinite ways of practicing Yoga. Certain methods have produced successful result with certain men. But two are of general importance with all: (1) Reaching the reality by negativing every known experience, (2) Thinking that you are everything, the whole universe. The second method, though it leads to the goal sooner than the first, is not the safest one. It is generally attended with great dangers which may lead a man astray and deter him from obtaining his aim.

There is this difference between the love taught by Christianity and that taught by Hinduism: Christianity teaches us to love our neighbours as we should wish them to love us; Hinduism asks us to love them as ourselves, in fact to see ourselves in them.

A mongoose is generally kept in a glass-case with a long chain attached to it, so that it may go about freely. When it scents danger as it wanders about, with one jump it goes into the glass-case. So is a Yogi in this world.

* * *

The whole universe is one chain of existence, of which matter forms one pole and God the other; the doctrine of Vishishtâdvaitism may be explained by some such ideas.

The Vedas are full of passages which prove the existence of a Personal God. The Rishis, who through long devotion saw God, had a peep into the unknown and threw their challenge to the world. It is only presumptuous men, who have not walked in the path described by the Rishis and who have not followed their teachings, that criticise them and oppose them. No man has yet come forward who would dare to say that he has properly followed their directions and has not seen anything and that these men are liars. There are men who have been under trial at various times and have felt that they have not been forsaken by God. The world is such that if faith in God does not offer us any consolation, it is better to commit suicide.

A pious missionary went out on business. All of a sudden his three sons died of cholera. His wife covered the three dead bodies of her beloved children with a sheet and was awaiting her husband at the gate. When he returned, she detained him at the gate and put him the question, "My dear husband, some one entrusts something to you and in your absence suddenly takes it back. Will you feel sorry?" He replied, "Certainly I would not".

Then she took him in, removed the sheet and showed the three corpses. He bore this calmly and buried the bodies. Such is the strength of mind of those who hold firm faith in the existence of an all-merciful God who disposes of everything in the universe.

The Absolute can never be thought of. We can have no idea of a thing unless it is finite. God the infinite can only be conceived and worshipped as the finite.

John the Baptist was an Essene — a sect of Buddhists. The Christian cross is nothing but the Shivalinga converted into two across. Remnants of Buddhist worship are still to be found among the relics of ancient Rome.

In South India, some of the Râgas (tunes) are sung and remembered as independent Ragas, whereas they are derivations of the six primary ones. In their music, there is very little of Murchhanâ, or oscillating touches of sound. Even the use of the perfect instrument of music is rare. The Vinâ of the South is not the real Vina. We have no martial music, no martial poetry either. Bhavabhuti is a little martial.

* * *

Christ was a Sannyâsin, and his religion is essentially fit for Sannyasins only. His teachings may be summed up as: "Give up"; nothing more — being fit for the favoured few.

"Turn the other cheek also!" — impossible, impracticable! The Westerners know it. It is meant for those who hunger and thirst after righteousness, who aim at perfection.

"Stand on your rights", is the rule for the ordinary men. One set of moral rules cannot be preached to all — Sâdhus and householders.

All sectarian religions take for granted that all men are equal. This is not warranted by science. There is more difference between minds than between bodies. One fundamental doctrine of Hinduism is that all men are different, there being unity in variety. Even for a drunkard, there are some Mantras — even for a man going to a prostitute!

Morality is a relative term. Is there anything like absolute morality in this world? The idea is a superstition. We have no right to judge every man in every age by the same standard.

Every man, in every age, in every country is under peculiar circumstances. If the circumstances change, ideas also must change. Beef-eating was once moral. The climate was cold, and the cereals were not much known. Meat was the chief food available. So in that age and clime, beef was in a manner indispensable. But beef-eating is held to be immoral now.

The one thing unchangeable is God. Society is moving. Jagat (world) means that which is moving. God is Achala (immovable).

What I say is not, "Reform", but, "Move on". Nothing is too bad to reform. Adaptability is the whole mystery of life — the principle underneath which serves to unfold it. Adjustment or adaptation is the outcome of the Self pitted against external forces tending to suppress It. He who adjusts himself best lives the longest. Even if I do not preach this, society is changing, it must change. It is not Christianity nor science, it is necessity, that is working underneath, the necessity that people must have to live or starve.

* * *

The best scenery in the world can be seen on the sublime heights of the Himalayas. If one lives there for a time, he is sure to have mental calmness, however restless he might have been before.

God is the highest form of generalised law. When once this law is known, all others can be explained as being subordinate to it. God is to religion what Newton's law of gravity is to falling bodies.

Every worship consists of prayer in the highest form. For a man who cannot make Dhyâna or mental worship, Pujâ or ceremonial worship is necessary. He must have the thing concrete.

The brave alone can afford to be sincere. Compare the lion and the fox.

Loving only the *good* in God and nature — even a child does that. You should love the terrible and the painful as well. A father loves the child, even when he is giving him trouble.

Shri Krishna was God, incarnated to save mankind. Gopi-Lilâ (his disport with the cowherd maids) is the acme of the religion of love in which individuality vanishes and there is communion. It is in this Lila that Shri Krishna shows what he preaches in the Gitâ: "Give up every other tie for me." Go and take shelter under Vrindâvana-Lila to understand Bhakti. On this subject a great number of books is extant. It is the religion of India. The larger number of Hindus follow Shri Krishna.

Shri Krishna is the God of the poor, the beggar, the the sinner, the son, the father, the wife, and of everyone. He enters intimately into all our human relations and makes everything holy and in the end brings us to salvation. He is the God who hides himself from the philosopher and the learned and reveals himself to the ignorant and the children. He is the God of faith and love and not of learning. With the Gopis, love and God were the same thing — they knew Him to be love incarnate.

In Dwârakâ, Shri Krishna teaches duty; in Vrindavana, love. He allowed his sons to kill each other, they being wicked.

God, according to the Jewish and Mohammedan idea, is a big Sessions Judge. Our God is rigorous on the surface, but loving and merciful at heart.

There are some who do not understand Advaitism and make a travesty of its teachings. They say, "What is Shuddha and Ashuddha (pure and impure) — what is the difference between virtue and vice? It is all human superstition", and observe no moral restraint in their actions. It is downright roguery; and any amount of harm is done by the preaching of such things.

This body is made up of two sorts of Karma consisting of virtue and vice — injurious vice and non-injurious virtue. A thorn is pricking my body, and I take another thorn to take it out and then throw both away. A man desiring to be perfect takes a thorn of virtue and with it takes off the thorn of vice. He still lives, and virtue alone being left, the momentum of action left to him must be of virtue. A bit of holiness is left to the Jivanmukta, and he lives, but everything he does must be holy.

Virtue is that which tends to our improvement, and vice to our degeneration. Man is made up of three qualities — brutal, human, and godly. That which tends to increase the divinity in you is virtue, and that which tends to increase brutality in you is vice. You must kill the brutal nature and become human, that is, loving and charitable. You must transcend that too and become pure bliss. Sachchidânanda, fire without burning, wonderfully loving, but without the weakness of human love, without the feeling of misery.

Bhakti is divided into Vaidhi and Râgânugâ Bhakti.

Vaidhi Bhakti is implicit belief in obedience to the teachings of the Vedas.

Raganuga Bhakti is of five kinds:

(1) Shânta as illustrated by the religion of Christ; (2) Dâsya as illustrated by that of Hanumân to Râma; (3) Sakhya as illustrated by that of Arjuna to Shri Krishna; (4) Vâtsalya as illustrated by that of Vasudeva to Shri Krishna; (5) Madhura (that of the husband and wife) in the lives of Shri Krishna and Gopikâs.

Keshab Chandra Sen compared society to an ellipse. God is the central sun. Society is sometimes in the aphelion and sometimes in the perihelion. An Avatâra comes and takes it to the perihelion. Then it goes back again. Why should it be so? I cannot say. What necessity for an Avatara? What necessity was there to create? Why did He not create us all perfect? It is Lilâ (sport), we do not know.

Men can become Brahman but not God. If anybody becomes God, show me his creation. Vishvâmitra's creation is his own imagination. It should have obeyed Vishvamitra's law. If anybody becomes a Creator, there would be an end of the world, on account of the conflict of laws. The balance is so nice that if you disturb the equilibrium of one atom, the whole world will come to an end.

There were great men — so great that no number nor human arithmetic could state the difference between them and us. But compared with God, they were geometrical points. In comparison with the Infinite, everything is nothing. Compared with God, what is Vishvamitra but a human moth?

Patanjali is the father of the theory of evolution, spiritual and physical.

Generally the organism is weaker than the environment. It is struggling to adjust itself. Sometimes it over-adjusts itself. Then the whole body changes into another species. Nandi was a man whose holiness was so great that the human body could not contain it. So those molecules changed into a god-body.

The tremendous engine of competition will destroy everything. If you are to live at all, you must adjust yourself to the times. If we are to live at all, we must be a scientific nation. Intellectual power is the force. You must learn the power of organisation of the Europeans. You must become educated and must educate your women. You must abolish child marriage.

All these ideas are floating over society. You all know it, yet dare not act. Who is to bell the cat? In the fullness of time a wonderful man will come. Then all the rats will be made bold.

Whenever a great man comes, the circumstances are ready under his feet. He is the last straw to break the camel's back. He is the spark of the cannon. There is something in the talking — we are preparing for him.

Was Krishna cunning? No, he was not cunning. He tried his best to prevent the war. It was Duryodhana who forced the war. But, when once in the thing, you should not recede — that is the man of duty. Do not run away, it is cowardice. When in the thing, you must do it. You should not budge an inch — of course not for a wrong thing; this war was a righteous war.

The devil comes in many guises — anger in the form of justice — passion in the form of duty. When it first comes, the man knows and then he forgets. Just as your pleaders' conscience; at first they know it is all Badmâshi (roguery), then it is duty to their clients; at last they get hardened.

Yogis live on the banks of the Narmada — the best place for them, because the climate is very even. Bhaktas live in Vrindâvana.

Sipâhis (sepoys) die soon — nature is full of defect — the athletes die soon. The gentlemen class are the strongest, while the poor are the hardiest. Fruit diet may agree with a costive man. Civilised man needs rest for intellectual work. For food he has to take spices and condiments. The savage walks forty or fifty miles a day. He relishes the blandest foods.

Our fruits are all artificial, and the natural mango is a poor affair. Wheat also is artificial.

Save the spiritual store in your body observing continence.

The rule for a householder about the expenditure of his income is, one-fourth of the income for his family, one-fourth for charity, one-fourth to be saved, one-fourth for self.

Unity in variety is the plan of creation, individuality in universality.

Why deny the cause only? Deny the effect also. The cause must contain everything that is in the effect.

Christ's public life extended only over eighteen months, and for this he had silently been preparing himself for thirty-two years.

Mohammed was forty years old before he came out.

* * *

It is true that the caste system becomes essential in the ordinary course of nature. Those that have aptitudes for a particular work form a class. But who is to settle the class of a particular individual? If a Brâhmin thinks that he has a special aptitude for spiritual culture, why should he be afraid to meet a Shudra in an open field? Will a horse be afraid of running a race with a jade?

Refer to the life of the author of *Krishna-karnâmrita*, Vilvamangala — a devotee who plucked his eyes out because he could not see God. His life illustrates the principle that even misdirected love leads in the end to love proper.

Too early religious advancement of the Hindus and that superfineness in everything which made them cling to higher alternatives, have reduced them to what they are. The Hindus have to learn a little bit of materialism from the West and teach them a little bit of spirituality.

Educate your women first and leave them to themselves; then they will tell you what reforms are necessary for them. In matters concerning them, who are you?

Who reduced the Bhângis and the Pariahs to their present degraded condition? Heartlessness in our behaviour and at the same time preaching wonderful Advaitism — is it not adding insult to injury?

Form and formless are intertwined in this world. The formless can only be expressed in form and form can only be thought with the formless. The world is a form of our thoughts. The idol is the expression of religion.

In God all natures are possible. But we can see Him only through human nature. We can love Him as we love a man — as father, son. The strongest love in the world is that between man and woman, and that also when it is clandestine. This is typified in the love between Krishna and Râdhâ.

Nowhere is it said in the Vedas that man is born a sinner. To say so is a great libel on human nature.

It is not an easy task to reach the state of seeing the Reality face to face. The other day one could not find the hidden cat in a whole picture, though it occupied the major portion of the picture.

* * *

You cannot injure anybody and sit quietly. It is a wonderful machinery — you cannot escape God's vengeance.

Kâma (lust) is blind and leads to hell. Prema is love, it leads to heaven.

There is no idea of lust or sympathy in the love of Krishna and Radha. Radha says to Krishna. "If you place sour feet on my heart, all lust will vanish."

When abstraction is reached lust dies and there is only love.

A poet loved a washerwoman. Hot Dâl fell upon the feet of the woman and the feet of the poet were scalded.

Shiva is the sublime aspect of God, Krishna the beautiful aspect of God. Love crystallises into blueness. Blue colour is expressive of intense love. Solomon saw "Krishna". Here Krishna came to be seen by all.

Even now, when you get love, you see Radha. Become Radha and be saved. There is no other way, Christians do not understand Solomon's song. They call it prophecy symbolising Christ's love for the Church. They think it nonsense and father some story upon it.

Hindus believe Buddha to be an Avatara.

Hindus believe in God positively. Buddhism does not try to know whether He is or not.

Buddha came to whip us into practice. Be good, destroy the passions. Then you will know for yourself whether Dvaita or Advaita philosophy is true — whether there is one or there are more than one.

Buddha was a reformer of Hinduism.

In the same man the mother sees a son, while the wife at the same time sees differently with different results. The wicked see in God wickedness. The virtuous see in Him virtue. He admits of all forms. He can be moulded according to the imagination of each person. Water assumes various shapes in various vessels. But water is in all of them. Hence all religions are true.

God is cruel and not cruel. He is all being and not being at the same time. Hence He is all contradictions. Nature also is nothing but a mass of contradictions.

* * *

Freedom of the will — it is as you feel you are free to act. But this freedom is a species of necessity. There is one infinite link before, after, and between the thought and the action but the latter takes the name of freedom — like a bird flitting through a bright room. We feel the freedom and feel it has no other cause. We cannot go beyond consciousness, therefore we feel we are free. We can trace it no further than consciousness. God alone feels the real freedom. Mahâpurushas (saints) feel themselves identified with God; hence they also feel the real freedom.

You may stop the water flowing out of the fountain by closing that part of the stream and gathering it all in the fountain; you have no liberty beyond it. But the source remains unchanged. Everything is predestination — and a part of that predestination is that you shall have such feeling — the feeling of freedom. I am shaping my own action. Responsibility is the feeling of reaction. There is no absolute power. Power here is the conscious feeling of exercising any faculty which is created by necessity. Man has the feeling "I act"; what he means by power of freedom is the feeling. The power is attended with responsibility. Whatever may be done through us by predestination, we feel the reaction. A ball thrown by one, itself feels the reaction.

But this innate necessity which comes to us as our freedom does not affect also the conscious relations we form with our surroundings. The relativity is not changed. Either everybody is free or everybody is under necessity. That would not matter. The relations would be the same. Vice and virtue would be the same. If a thief pleads that he was under the necessity of stealing, the magistrate would say that he was under the necessity to punish. We are seated in a room, and the whole room is moving — the relation between us is unchanged. To get out of this infinite chain of causation is Mukti (freedom). Muktas (free souls) are not actuated by necessity, they are like god. They begin the chain of cause and effect. God is the only free being — the first source of their will — and is always experienced by them as such.

The feeling of want is the real prayer, not the words. But you must have patience to wait and see if your prayers are answered.

You should cultivate a noble nature by doing your duty. By doing our duty we get rid of the idea of duty; and then and then only we feel everything as done by God. We are but machines in His hand. This body is opaque, God is the lamp. Whatever is going out of the body is God's. You do not feel it. You feel "I". This is delusion. You must learn calm submission to the will of God. Duty is the best school for it. This duty is morality. Drill yourself to be thoroughly submissive. Get rid of the "I". No humbuggism. Then you can get rid of the idea of duty; for all is His. Then you go on naturally, forgiving, forgetting, etc.

Our religion always presents different gradations of duty and religion to different people.

Light is everywhere visible only in the men of holiness. A Mahapurusha is like crystal glass — full rays of God passing and repassing through. Why not worship a Jivanmukta?

Contact with holy men is good. If you go near holy men, you will field holiness overflowing unconsciously in everything there.

Resist not evil done to yourself, but you may resist evil done to others.

If you wish to become a saint, you should renounce all kinds of pleasures. Ordinarily, you may enjoy all, but pray to God for guidance, and He will lead you on.

The universe fills only a small portion of the heart which craves for something beyond and above the world.

Selfishness is the devil incarnate in every man. Every bit of self, bit by bit, is devil. Take off self by one side and God enters by the other. When the self is got rid of, only God remains. Light and darkness cannot remain together.

Forgetting the little "I" is a sign of healthy and pure mind. A healthy child forgets its body.

Sitâ — to say that she was pure is a blasphemy. She was purity itself embodied — the most beautiful character that ever lived on earth.

A Bhakta should be like Sita before Râma. He might be thrown into all kinds of difficulties. Sita did not mind her sufferings; she centred herself in Rama.

* * *

Buddhism proves nothing about the Absolute Entity. In a stream the water is changing; we have no right to call the stream *one*. Buddhists deny the *one*, and say, it is *many*. We say it is *one* and deny the *many*. What they call Karma is what we call the soul. According to Buddhism, man is a series of waves. Every wave dies, but somehow the first wave causes the second. That the second wave is identical with the first is illusion. To get rid of illusion good Karma is necessary. Buddhists do not postulate anything beyond the world. We say, beyond the relative there is the Absolute. Buddhism accepts that there is misery, and sufficient it is that we can get rid of this Dukkha (misery); whether we get Sukha (happiness) or not, we do not know. Buddha preached not the soul preached by others. According to the Hindus, soul is an entity or substance, and God is absolute. Both agree in this, that they destroy the relative. But Buddhists duo not give what is the effect of that destruction of the relative.

Present-day Hinduism and Buddhism were growths from the same branch. Buddhism degenerated, and Shankara lopped it off!

Buddha is said to have denied the Vedas because there is so much Himsâ (killing) and other things. Every page of Buddhism is a fight with the Vedas (the ritualistic aspect). But he had no authority to do so.

Buddha is expressly agnostic about God; but God is everywhere preached in our religion. The Vedas teach God — both personal and impersonal. God is everywhere preached in the Gitâ. Hinduism is nothing without God. The Vedas are nothing without Him. That is the only way to salvation. Sannyâsins have to repeat the following, several times: I, wishing for Mukti, take refuge in God, who created the world, who breathed out the Vedas.

Buddha, we may say now, ought to have understood the harmony of religions. He introduced sectarianism.

Modern Hinduism, modern Jainism, and Buddhism branched off at the same time. For some period, each seemed to have wanted to outdo the others in grotesqueness and humbuggism.

* * *

We cannot imagine anything which is not God. He is all that we can imagine with our five senses, and more. He is like a chameleon; each man, each nation, sees one face of Him and at different times, in different forms. Let each man see and take of God whatever is suitable to him. Compare each animal absorbing from nature whatever food is suitable to it.

The fault with all religions like Christianity is that they have one set of rules for all. But Hindu religion is suited to all grades of religious aspiration and progress. It contains all the ideals in their perfect form. For example, the ideal of Shânta or blessedness is to be found in Vasishtha; that of love in Krishna; that of duty in Rama and Sita; and that of intellect in Shukadeva. Study the characters of these and of other ideal men. Adopt one which suits you best.

Follow truth wherever it may lead you; carry ideas to their utmost logical conclusions. Do not be cowardly and hypocritical. You must have a great devotion to your ideal, devotion not of the moment, but calm, persevering, and steady devotion, like that of a Châtaka (a kind of bird) which looks into the sky in the midst of thunder and lightning and would drink no water but from the clouds. Perish in the struggle to be holy; a thousand times welcome death. Be not disheartened. When good nectar is unattainable, it is no reason why we should eat poison. There is no escape. *This* world is as unknown as the other.

Charity never faileth; devotion to an ideal never fails in sympathy, never becomes weary of sympathising with others. Love to enemies is not possible for ordinary men: they drive out others in order to live themselves. Only a very few men lived in the world who practiced both. King Janaka was one of them. Such a man is superior even to Sannyasins. Shukadeva, who was purity and renunciation embodied, made Janaka his Guru; and Janaka said to him, "You are a born Siddha; whatever you know and your father taught you, is true. I assure you of this."

* * *

Individuality in universality is the plan of creation. Each cell has its part in bringing about consciousness. Man is individual and at the same time universal. It is while realising our individual nature that we realise even our national and universal nature. Each is an infinite circle whose centre is everywhere and circumference nowhere. By practice one can feel universal Selfhood which is the essence of Hinduism. He who sees in every being his own Self is a Pandita (sage).

Rishis are discoverers of spiritual laws.

In Advaitism, there is no Jivâtmâ; it is only a delusion. In Dvaitism, there is Jiva infinitely distinct from God. Both are true. One went to the fountain, another to the tank. Apparently we are all Dvaitists as far as our consciousness goes. But beyond? Beyond that we are Advaitists. In reality, this is the only truth. According to Advaitism, love every man as your own Self and not as your brother as in Christianity. Brotherhood should be superseded by universal Selfhood. Not universal brotherhood, but universal Selfhood is our motto. Advaitism may include also the "greatest happiness" theory.

So'ham — I am He. Repeat the idea constantly, voluntarily at first; then it becomes automatic in practice. It percolates to the nerves. So this idea, by rote, by repetition, should be driven even into the nerves.

Or, first begin with Dvaitism that is in your consciousness; second stage, Vishishtâdvaitism — "I in you, you in me, and all is God." This is the teaching of Christ.

The highest Advaitism cannot be brought down to practical life. Advaitism made practical works from the plane of Vishishtadvaitism. Dvaitism — small circle different from the big circle, only connected by Bhakti; Vishishtadvaitism — small circle within big circle, motion regulated by the big circle; Advaitism — small circle expands and coincides with the big circle. In Advaitism "I" loses itself in God. God is here, God is there, God is "I".

* * *

One way for attaining Bhakti is by repeating the name of God a number of times. Mantras have effect — the mere repetition of words. Jalangiman Chetti's powers are due to the repetition of the Mantra — repetition of certain words with certain ceremonies. The powers of the Astras or Bânas (missiles, arrows, etc.) of ancient war were due to Mantra. This is taken for granted throughout our Shâstras. That we should take all these Shastras to be imagination is superstition.

To obtain Bhakti, seek the company of holy men who have Bhakti, and read books like the Gita and the *Imitation of Christ*; always think of the attributes of God.

The Vedas contain not only the means how to obtain Bhakti but also the means for obtaining any earthly good or evil. Take whatever you want.

Bengal is a land of Bhakti or Bhaktas. The stone on which Chaitanya used to stand in the temple of Jagannâtha to see the image was worn by his tears of love and devotion. When he took Sannyâsa, he showed his fitness for it to his Guru by keeping sugar on his tongue for some time without its being dissolved. He discovered Vrindavana by the power of insight he had acquired through devotion.

I will tell you something for your guidance in life. Everything that comes from India take as true, until you find cogent reasons for disbelieving it. Everything that. comes from Europe take as false, until you find cogent reasons for believing it. Do not be carried away by European fooleries. Think for yourselves. Only one thing is lacking: you are slaves; you follow whatever Europeans do. That is simply an impotent state of mind. Society may take up materials from any quarter but should grow in its own way.

To be shocked by a new custom is the father of all Superstition, the first road to hell. It leads to bigotry and fanaticism. Truth is heaven. Bigotry is hell.

Concentration

Concentration is the essence of all knowledge, nothing can be done without it. Ninety per cent of thought force is wasted by the ordinary human being, and therefore he is constantly committing blunders; the trained man or mind never makes a mistake. When the mind is concentrated and turned backward on itself, all within us will be our servants, not our masters. The Greeks applied their concentration to the external world, and the result was perfection in art, literature, etc. The Hindu concentrated on the internal world, upon the unseen realms in the Self, and developed the science of Yoga. Yoga is controlling the senses, will and mind. The benefit of its study is that we learn to control instead of being controlled. Mind seems to be layer on layer. Our real goal is to cross all these intervening strata of our being and find God. The end and aim of Yoga is to realise God. To do this we must go beyond relative knowledge, go beyond the sense-world. The world is awake to the senses, the children of the Lord are asleep on that plane. The world is asleep to the Eternal, the children of the Lord are awake in that realm. These are the sons of God. There is but one way to control the senses — to see Him who is the Reality in the universe. Then and only then can we really conquer our senses.

Concentration is restraining the mind into smaller and smaller limits. There are eight processes for thus restraining the mind. The first is Yama, controlling the mind by avoiding externals. All morality is included in this. Beget no evil. Injure no living creature. If you injure nothing for twelve years, then even lions and tigers will go down before you. Practise truthfulness. Twelve years of absolute truthfulness in thought, word, and deed gives a man what he wills. Be chaste in thought, word, and action. Chastity is the basis of all religions. Personal purity is imperative. Next is Niyama, not allowing the mind to wander in any direction. Then Âsana, posture. There are eighty-four postures: but the best is that most natural to each one; that is, which can be kept longest with the greatest ease. After this comes Prânâyâma, restraint of breath. Then Pratyâhâra, drawing in of the organs from their objects. Then Dhâranâ, concentration. Then Dhyâna, contemplation or meditation. (This is the kernel of the Yoga system.) And last, Samâdhi, superconsciousness. The purer the body and mind, the quicker the desired result will be obtained. You must be perfectly pure. Do not think of evil things, such thoughts will surely drag you down. If you are perfectly pure and practice faithfully, your mind can finally be made a searchlight of infinite power. There is no limit to its scope. But there must be constant practice and non-attachment to the world. When a man reaches the superconscious state, all feeling of body melts away. Then alone does he become free and immortal. To all external appearance, unconsciousness and superconsciousness are the same; but they differ as a lump of clay from a lump of gold. The one whose whole soul is given up to God has reached the superconscious plane.

The Power Of The Mind

The cause becomes the effect. The cause is not one thing and the effect something else that exists as a result. The effect is always the cause worked out. Always, the cause becomes the effect. The popular idea is that the effect is the result of the operation of a cause which is something independent and aloof from the effect. al his is not so. The effect is always the cause worked out into another condition.

The universe is really homogeneous. Heterogeneity is only in appearance. There seem to be different substances, different powers, etc. throughout nature. But take two different substances, say a piece of glass and a piece of wood, grind them up together fine enough, reduce them till there is nothing more to reduce, and the substance remaining appears homogeneous. All substances in the last analysis are one. Homogeneity is the substance, the reality; heterogeneity is the appearance of many things as though they were mans' substances. The One is homogeneity; the appearance of the One as many is heterogeneity.

Hearing, seeing, or tasting, etc. is the mind in different states of action.

The atmosphere of a room may be hypnotised so that everybody who enters it will see all sorts of things — men and objects flying through the air.

Everybody is hypnotised already. The work of attaining freedom, of realising one's real nature, consists in de-hypnotisation. One thing to be remembered is that we are not gaining powers at all. We have them already. The whole process of growth is de-hypnotisation.

The purer the mind, the easier it is to control. Purity of the mind must be insisted upon if you would control it. Do not think covetously about mere mental powers. Let them go. One who seeks the powers of the mind succumbs to them. Almost all who desire powers become ensnared by them.

Perfect morality is the all in all of complete control over mind. The man who is perfectly moral has nothing more to do; he is free. The man who is perfectly moral cannot possibly hurt anything or anybody. Non-injuring has to be attained by him who would be free. No one is more powerful than he who has attained perfect non-injuring. No one could fight, no one could quarrel, in his presence. Yes, his very presence, and nothing else, means peace, means love wherever he may be. Nobody could be angry or fight in his presence. Even the animals, ferocious animals, would be peaceful before him.

I once knew a Yogi, a very old man, who lived in a hole in the ground all by himself. (Pavhâri Bâbâ of Ghazipur. (See Vol. IV.)) All he had was a pan or two to cook his meals in. He ate very little, and wore scarcely anything, and spent most of his time meditating.

With him all people were alike. He had attained to non-injuring. What he saw in everything, in every person, in every animal, was the Soul, the Lord of the Universe. With him, every person and every animal was "my Lord". He never addressed any person or animal in any other way. Well, one day a thief came his way and stole one of his pans. He saw him and ran after him. The chase was a long one. At last the thief from exhaustion had to stop, and the Yogi, running up to him, fell on his knees before him and said, "My Lord, you do me a great honour to come my way. Do me the honour to accept the other pan. It is also yours." This old man is dead now. He was full of love for everything in the world. He would have died for an ant. Wild animals instinctively knew this old man to be their friend. Snakes and ferocious animals would go into his hole and sleep with him. They all loved him and never fought in his presence.

Never talk about the faults of others, no matter how bad they may be. Nothing is ever gained by that. You never help one by talking about his fault; you do him an injury, and injure yourself as well.

All regulations in eating, practicing, etc., are all right so long as they are complementary to a spiritual aspiration but they are not ends in themselves; they are only helps.

Never quarrel about religion. All quarrels and disputations concerning religion simply show that spirituality is not present. Religious quarrels are always over the husks. When purity, when spirituality goes, leaving the soul dry, quarrels begin, and not before.

Lessons On Raja-Yoga

(These lessons and those on Bhakti-Yoga that follow are made out of class notes preserved in England — Ed.)

PRANA

The theory of creation is that matter is subject to five conditions: ether, luminous ether, gaseous, liquid, and solid. They are all evoked out of one primal element, which is very finest ether.

The name of the energy in the universe is Prâna, which is the force residing in these elements. Mind is the great instrument for using the Prana. Mind is material. Behind the mind is Âtman which takes hold of the Prana. Prana is the driving power of the world, and can be seen in every manifestation of life. The body is mortal and the mind is mortal; both, being compounds, must die. Behind all is the Atman which never dies. The Atman is pure intelligence controlling and directing Prana. But the intelligence we see around us is always imperfect. When intelligence is perfect, we get the Incarnation — the Christ. Intelligence is always trying to manifest itself, and in order to do this it is creating minds and bodies of different degrees of development. In reality, and at the back of all things, every being is equal.

Mind is very fine matter; it is the instrument for manifesting Prana. Force requires matter for manifestation.

The next point is how to use this Prana. We all use it, but how sadly we waste it! The first doctrine in the preparatory stage is that all knowledge is the outcome of experience. Whatever is beyond the five senses must also be experienced in order to become true to us.

Our mind is acting on three planes: the subconscious, conscious, and superconscious. Of men, the Yogi alone is superconscious. The whole theory of Yoga is to go beyond the mind. These three planes can be understood by considering the vibrations of light or sound. There are certain vibrations of light too slow to become visible; then as they get faster, we see them as light; and then they get too fast for us to see them at all. The same with sound.

How to transcend the senses without disturbing the health is what we want to learn. The Western mind has stumbled into acquiring some of the psychic gifts which in them are abnormal and are frequently the sign of disease. The Hindu has studied and made perfect this subject of science, which all may now study without fear or danger.

Mental healing is a fine proof of the superconscious state; for the thought which heals is a sort of vibration in the Prana, and it does not go as a thought but as something higher for which we have no name.

Each thought has three states. First, the rising or beginning, of which we are unconscious; second, when the thought rises to the surface; and third, when it goes from us. Thought is like a bubble rising to the surface. When thought is joined to will, we call it power. That which strikes the sick person whom you are trying to help is not thought, but power. The self-man running through it all is called in Sanskrit Sutrâtmâ, the "Thread-self".

The last and highest manifestation of Prana is love. The moment you have succeeded in manufacturing love out of Prana, you are free. It is the hardest and the greatest thing to gain. You must not criticise others; you must criticise *yourself.* If you see a drunkard, do not criticise him; remember he is you in another shape. He who has not darkness sees no darkness in others. What you have inside you is that you see in others. This is the surest way of reform. If the would-be reformers who criticise and see evil would themselves stop creating evil, the world would be better. Beat this idea into yourself.

THE PRACTICE OF YOGA

The body must be properly taken care of. The people who torture their flesh are demoniacal. Always keep your mind joyful; if melancholy thoughts come, kick them out. A Yogi must not eat too much, but he also must not fast; he must not sleep too much, but he must not go without any sleep. In all things only the man who holds the golden mean can become a Yogi.

What is the best time for practice in Yoga? The junction time of dawn and twilight, when all nature becomes calm. Take help of nature. Take the easiest posture in sitting. Have the three parts straight — the ribs, the shoulders, and the head — leaving the spine free and straight, no leaning backwards or forwards. Then mentally hold the body as perfect, part by part. Then send a current of love to all the world; then pray for enlightenment. And lastly, join your mind to your breath and gradually attain the power of concentrating your attention on its movements. The reason for this will be apparent by degrees.

THE OJAS

The "Ojas" is that which makes the difference between man and man. The man who has much Ojas is the leader of men. It gives a tremendous power of attraction. Ojas is manufactured from the nerve-currents. It has this peculiarity: it is most easily made from that force which manifests itself in the sexual powers. If the powers of the sexual centres are not frittered away and their energies wasted (action is only thought in a grosser state), they can be manufactured into Ojas. The two great nerve-currents of the body start from the brain, go down on each side of the spinal cord, but they cross in the shape of the figure 8 at the back of the head. Thus the left side of the body is governed by the right side of the head. At the lowest point of the circuit is the sexual centre, the Sacral Plexus. The energy conveyed by these two currents of nerves comes down, and a large amount is continually being stored in the Sacral Plexus. The last bone in the spine is over the Sacral Plexus and is described in symbolic language as a triangle; and as the energy is stored up beside it, this energy is symbolised by a serpent. Consciousness and subconsciousness work through these two nerve-currents. But superconsciousness takes off the nerve-current when it reaches the lower end of the circuit, and instead of allowing it to go up and complete the circuit, stops and forces it up the spinal cord as Ojas from the Sacral Plexus. The spinal cord is naturally closed, but it can be opened to form a passage for this Ojas. As the current travels from one centre of the spinal cord to another, *you* can travel from one plane of existence to another. This is why the human being is greater than others, because all planes, all experiences, are possible to the spirit in the human body. We do not need another; for man can, if he likes, finish in his body his probation and can after that become pure spirit. When the Ojas has gone from centre to centre and reaches the Pineal Gland (a part of the brain to which science can assign no function), man then becomes neither mind nor body, he is free from all bondage.

The great danger of psychic powers is that man stumbles, as it were, into them, and knows not how to use them rightly. He is without training and without knowledge of what has happened to him. The danger is that in using these psychic powers, the sexual feelings are abnormally roused as these powers are in fact manufactured out of the sexual centre. The best and safest way is to avoid psychic manifestations, for they play the most horrible pranks on their ignorant and untrained owners.

To go back to symbols. Because this movement of the Ojas up the spinal cord feels like a spiral one, it is called the "snake". The snake, therefore, or the serpent, rests on the bone or triangle. When it is roused, it travels up the spinal cord; and as it goes from centre to centre, a new natural world is opened inside us — the Kundalini is roused.

PRANAYAMA

The practice of Pranayama is the training of the superconscious mind. The physical practice is divided into three parts and deals entirely with the breath. It consists of drawing in, holding, and throwing out the breath. The breath must be drawn in by one nostril whilst you count four, then held whilst you count sixteen, and thrown away by the other nostril whilst you count eight. Then reverse the process closing the other nostril while you breathe in. You will have to begin by holding one nostril with your thumb; but in time your breathing will obey your mind. Make four of these Pranayamas morning and evening.

METAGNOSTICISM

"Repent, for the Kingdom of Heaven is at hand." The word "repent" is in Greek "metanoeite" ("meta" means behind, after, beyond) and means literally "go beyond knowledge — the knowledge of the (five) senses — "and look within where you will find the kingdom of heaven".

Sir William Hamilton says at the end of a philosophical work, "Here philosophy ends, here religion begins". Religion is not, and never can be, in the field of intellect. Intellectual reasoning is based on facts evident to the senses. Now religion has nothing to do with the *senses*. The agnostics say they cannot know God, and rightly, for they have exhausted the limits of their senses and yet get no further in knowledge of God. Therefore in order to prove religion — that is, the existence of God, immortality, etc. — we have to go beyond the knowledge of the senses. All great prophets and seers claim to have "seen God", that is to say, they have had direct experience. There is no knowledge without experience, and man has to see God in his own soul. When man has come face to face with the one great fact in the universe, then alone will doubts vanish and crooked things become straight. This is "seeing God". Our business is to verify, not to swallow. Religion, like other sciences, requires you to gather facts, to see for yourself, and this is possible when you go beyond the knowledge which lies in the region of the five senses. Religious truths need verification by everyone. To see God is the one goal. Power is not the goal. Pure Existence-Knowledge and Love is the goal; and Love is God.

THOUGHT, IMAGINATION, AND MEDITATION

The same faculty that we employ in dreams and thoughts, namely, imagination, will also be the means by which we arrive at Truth. When the imagination is very powerful, the object becomes visualised. Therefore by it we can bring our bodies to any state of health or disease. When we see a thing, the particles of the brain fall into a certain position like the mosaics of a kaleidoscope. Memory consists in getting back this combination and the same setting of the particles of the brain. The stronger the will, the greater will be the success in resetting these particles of the brain. There is only one power to cure the body, and that is in every man. Medicine only rouses this power. Disease is only the manifest struggle of that power to throw off the poison which has entered the body. Although the power to overthrow poison may be roused by medicine, it may be snore permanently roused by the force of thought. Imagination must hold to the thought of health and strength in order that in case of illness the memory of the ideal of health may be roused and the particles re-arranged in the position into which they fell when healthy. The tendency of the body is then to follow the brain.

The next step is when this process can be arrived at by another's mind working on us. Instances of this may be seen every day. Words are only a mode of mind acting on mind. Good and evil thoughts are each a potent power, and they fill the universe. As vibration continues so thought remains in the form of thought until translated into action. For example, force is latent in the man's arm until he strikes a blow, when he translates it into activity. We are the heirs of good and evil thought. If we make ourselves pure and the instruments of good thoughts, these will enter us. The good soul will not be receptive to evil thoughts. Evil thoughts find the best field in evil people; they are like microbes which germinate and increase only when they find a suitable soil. Mere thoughts are like little waveless; fresh impulses to vibration come to them simultaneously, until at last one great wave seems to stand up and swallow up the rest. These universal thought-waves seem to recur every five hundred years, when invariably the great wave typifies and swallows up the others. It is this which constitutes a prophet. He focuses in his own mind the thought of the age in which he is living and gives it back to mankind in concrete form. Krishna, Buddha, Christ, Mohammed, and Luther may be instanced as the great waves that stood up above their fellows (with a probable lapse of five hundred years between them). Always the wave that is backed by the greatest purity and the noblest character is what breaks upon the world as a movement of social reform. Once again in our day there is a vibration of the waves of thought and the central idea is that of the Immanent God, and this is everywhere cropping up in every form and every sect. In these waves, construction alternates with destruction; yet the construction always makes an end of the work of destruction. Now, as a man dives deeper to reach his spiritual nature, he feels no longer bound by superstition. The majority of sects will be transient, and last only as bubbles because the leaders are not usually men of character. Perfect love, the heart never reacting, this is what builds character. There is no allegiance possible where there is no character in the leader, and perfect purity ensures the most lasting allegiance and confidence.

Take up an idea, devote yourself to it, struggle on in patience, and the sun will rise for you.

* * *

To return to imagination:

We have to visualise the Kundalini. The symbol is the serpent coiled on the triangular bone.

Then practice the breathing as described before, and, while holding the breath, imagine that breath like the current which flows down the figure 8; when it reaches the lowest point, imagine that it strikes the serpent on the triangle and causes the serpent to mount up the channel within the spinal cord. Direct the breath in thought to this triangle.

We have now finished the physical process and from this point it becomes mental.

The first exercise is called the "gathering-in". The mind has to be gathered up or withdrawn from wandering.

After the physical process, let the mind run on and do not restrain it; but keep watch on your mind as a witness watching its action. This mind is thus divided into two — the player and the witness. Now strengthen the witnessing part and do not waste time in restraining your wanderings. The mind must think; but slowly and gradually, as the witness does its part, the player will come more and more under control, until at last you cease to play or wander.

2nd Exercise: Meditation — which may be divided into two. We are concrete in constitution and the mind must think in forms. Religion admits this necessity and gives the help of outward forms and ceremonies. You cannot meditate on God without some form. One will come to you, for thought and symbol are inseparable. Try to fix your mind on that form.

3rd Exercise: This is attained by practicing meditation and is really "one-pointedness". The mind usually works in a circle; make it remain on one point.

The last is the result. When the mind has reached this, all is gained — healing, clairvoyance, and all psychic gifts. In a moment you can direct this current of thought to anyone, as Jesus did, with instantaneous result.

People have stumbled upon these gifts without previous training, but I advise you to wait and practice all these steps slowly; then you will get everything under your control. You may practice healing a little if love is the motive, for that cannot hurt. Man is very short-sighted and impatient. All want power, but few will wait to gain it for themselves. He distributes but will not store up. It takes a long time to earn and but a short time to distribute. Therefore store up your powers as you acquire them and do not dissipate them.

Every wave of passion restrained is a balance in your favour. It is therefore good *policy* not to return anger for anger, as with all true morality. Christ said, "Resist not evil", and we do not understand it until we discover that it is not only moral but actually the best policy, for anger is loss of energy to the man who displays it. You should not allow your minds to come into those brain-combinations of anger and hatred.

When the primal element is discovered in chemical science, the work of the chemist will be finished. When unity is discovered, perfection in the science of religion is reached, and this was attained thousands of y ears ago. Perfect unity is reached when man says, "I and my Father are one".

Lessons On Bhakti-Yoga

THE YOGA THROUGH DEVOTION

We have been considering Raja-Yoga and the physical exercises. Now we shall consider Yoga through devotion. But you must remember that no one system is *necessary* (for all). I want to set before you many systems, many ideals, in order that you may find one that will suit you; if one does not, perhaps another may.

We want to become harmonious beings, with the psychical, spiritual, intellectual, and working (active) sides of our nature equally developed. Nations and individuals typify one of these sides or types and cannot understand more than that one. They get so built up into one ideal that they cannot see any other. The ideal is really that we should become many-sided. Indeed the cause of the misery of the world is that we are so one-sided that we cannot sympathise with one another. Consider a man looking at the sun from beneath the earth, up the shaft of a mine; he sees one aspect of the sun. Then another man sees the sun from the earth's level, another through mist and fog, another from the mountain top. To each the sun is a different appearance. So there are many appearances, but in reality there is only one sun. There is diversity of vision, but one object; and that is the sun.

Each man, according to his nature, has a peculiar tendency and takes to certain ideals and a certain path by which to reach them. But the goal is always the same to all. The Roman Catholic is deep and spiritual, but he has lost breadth. The Unitarian is wide, but he has lost spirituality and considers religion as of divided importance. What we want is the depth of the Roman Catholic and the breadth of the Unitarian. We must be as broad as the skies, as deep as the ocean; we must have the zeal of the fanatic, the depth of the mystic, and the width of the agnostic. The word "toleration" has acquired an unpleasant association with the conceited man who, thinking himself in a high position, looks down on his fellow-creatures with pity This is a horrible state of mind. We are all travelling the same way, towards the same goal, but by different paths made by the necessities of the case to suit diverse minds. We must become many-sided, indeed we must become protean in character, so as not only to tolerate, but to do what its much more difficult, to sympathise, to enter into another's path, and feel *with him* in his aspirations and seeking; after God. There are two elements in every religion — a positive and a negative. In. Christianity, for instance, when you speak of the Incarnation, of the Trinity, of salvation through Jesus Christ, I am with you. I say, "Very good, that I also hold true." But when you go on to says, "There is no other true religion, there is no other revelation of God", then I say, "Stop, I cannot go with your when you shut out, when you deny." Every religion has a message to deliver, something to teach man; but when it begins to protest, when it tries to disturb others, then it takes up a negative and therefore a dangerous position, and does not know where to begin or where to end.

Every force completes a circuit. The force we call man starts from the Infinite God and must return to Him. This return to God must be accomplished in one of two ways — either by slowly drifting back, going with nature, or by our own inward power, which causes us to stop on our course, which would, if left alone, carry us in a circuit back to God, and violently turn round and find God, as it were, by a short cut. This is what the Yogi does.

I have said that every man must choose his own ideal which is in accord with his nature. This ideal is called a man's Ishta. You must keep, it sacred (and therefore secret) and when you worship God, worship according to your Ishta. How are we to find out the particular method? It is very difficult, but as you persevere in your worship, it will come of itself. Three things are the special gifts of God to man — the human body, the desire to be free, and the blessing of help from one who is already free. Now, we cannot have devotion without a Personal God. There must be the lover and the beloved. God is an infinitised human being. It is bound to be so, for so long as we are human, we must have a humanised God, we are forced to see a Personal God and Him only. Consider how all that we see in this world is not the object pure and simple, but the object *plus* our own mind. The chair plus the chair's reaction on your mind is the real chair. You must colour everything with your mind, and then alone you can see it. (Example: The white, square, shiny, hard box, seen by the man with three senses, then by the man with four senses, then by him with five senses. The last alone sees it with all the enumerated qualities, and each one before has seen an additional one to the previous man. Now suppose a man with six senses sees the same box, he would see still another quality added.)

Because I see love and knowledge, I know the universal cause is manifesting that love and knowledge. How can that be loveless which causes love in me? We cannot think of the universal cause without human qualities. To see God as separate from ourselves in the universe is necessary as a first step. There are three visions of God: the lowest vision, when God seems to have a body like ourselves (see Byzantine art); a higher vision when we invest God with human qualities; and then on and on, till we come to the highest vision, when we see God.

But remember that in *all* these steps we are seeing God and God alone; there is no illusion in it, no mistake. Just as when we saw the sun from different points, it was still the sun and not the moon or anything else.

We cannot help seeing God as we are — infinitised, but still as we are. Suppose we tried to conceive God as the Absolute, we should have again to come back to the relative state in order to enjoy and love.

The devotion to God as seen in every religion is divided into two parts: the devotion which works through forms and ceremonies and through words, and that which works through love. In this world we are bound by laws, and we are always striving to break through these laws, we are always trying to disobey, to trample on nature. For instance, nature gives us no houses, we build them. Nature made us naked, we clothe ourselves. Man's goal is to be free, and just in so far as we fare incompetent to break nature's laws shall we suffer. We only obey nature's law in order to be *outlawed* — beyond law. The whole struggle of life is *not* to obey. (That is why I sympathise with Christian Scientists, for they teach the liberty of man and the divinity of soul.) The soul is superior to all environment. "The universe is my father's kingdom; I am the heir-apparent" — that is the attitude for man to take. "My own soul can subdue all."

We must work through law before we come to liberty. External helps and methods, forms, ceremonies, creeds, doctrines, all have their right place and are meant to support and strengthen us *until we become strong*. Then they are no more necessary. They are our nurses, and as such indispensable in youth. Even books are nurses, medicines are nurses. But we must work to bring about the time when man shall recognise his mastery over his own body. Herbs and medicines have power over us as long as we allow them; when we become strong, these external methods are no more necessary.

WORSHIPS THROUGH WORDS AND LOVE

Body is only mind in a grosser form, mind being composed of finer layers and the body being the denser layers; and when man has perfect control over his mind, he will also have control over his body. Just as each mind has its own peculiar body, so to each word belongs a particular thought. We talk in double consonants when we are angry — "stupid", "fool", "idiot", etc., in soft vowels when we are sad — "Ah me!" These are momentary, feelings, of course; but there are eternal feelings, such as love, peace, calmness, joy, holiness; and these feelings have their word-expression in all religions, the word being only the embodiment of these, man's highest feelings. Now the thought has produced the word, and in their turn these words may produce the thoughts or feelings. This is where the help of words come in. Each of such words covers one ideal. These sacred mysterious words we all recognise and know, and yet if we merely read them in books, they have no effect on us. To be effective, they must be charged with spirit, touched and used by one who has himself been touched by the Spirit of God and who now *lives*. It is only he who can set the current in motion. The "laying on of hands" is the continuation of that current which was set in motion by Christ. The one who has the power of transmitting this current is called a Guru. With great teachers the use of words is not necessary — as with Jesus. But the "small fry" transmit this current through words.

Do not look on the faults of others. You cannot judge a man by his faults. (Example: Suppose we were to judge of an apple tree by the rotten, unripe, unformed apples we find on the ground. Even so do the faults of a man not show what the man's character is.) Remember, the wicked are always the same all over the world. The thief and the murderer are the same in Asia and Europe and America. They form a nation by themselves. It is only in the good and the pure and the strong that you find variety. Do not recognise wickedness in others. Wickedness is ignorance, weakness What is the good of telling people they are weak? Criticism and destruction are of no avail. We must give them something higher: tell them of their own glorious nature, their birthright. Why do not more people come to God? The reason is that so few people have any enjoyments outside their five senses. The majority *cannot* see with their eyes nor hear with their ears in the inner world.

We now come to Worship through Love.

It has been said, "It is good to be born in a church, but not to die in it." The tree receives support and shelter from the hedge that surrounds it when young; but unless the hedge is removed, the growth and strength of that tree will be hindered. Formal worship, as we have seen, is a necessary stage, but gradually by slow growth we outgrow it and come to a higher platform.

When love to God becomes perfect, we think no more of the qualities of God — that He is omnipotent, omnipresent, and all those big adjectives. We do not *want* anything of God, so we do not care to notice these qualities. Just all we want is love of God. But anthropomorphism still follows us. We cannot get away from our humanity, we cannot jump out of our bodies; so we must love God as we love one another.

There are five steps in human love.

1. The lowest, most commonplace, "peaceful" love, when we look up to our Father for all we want — protection, food, etc.

2. The love which makes us want to serve. Man wants to serve God as his master, the longing to serve dominating every other feeling; and we are indifferent whether the master is good or bad, kind or unkind.

3. The love of a friend, the love of equals — companions, playmates. Man feels God to be his companion.

4. Motherly love. God is looked upon as a child. In India this is considered a higher love than the foregoing, because it has absolutely no element of fear.

5. The love of husband and wife; love for love's sake — God the perfect, beloved one.

It has been beautifully expressed: "Four eyes meet, a change begins to come into two souls; love comes in the middle between these two souls and makes them *one*."

When a man has this last and most perfect form of love, then all desires vanish, forms and doctrines and churches drop away, even the desire for freedom (the end and aim of all religions is freedom from birth and death and other things) is given up. The highest love is the love that is sexless, for it is perfect unity that is expressed in the highest love, and sex differentiates bodies. It is therefore only in spirit that union is possible. The less we have of the physical idea, the more perfect will be our love; at last all physical thought will be forgotten, and the two souls will become one. We love, love always. Love comes and penetrates through the forms and sees beyond. It has been said, "The lover sees Helen's beauty in an Ethiopian's brow." The Ethiopian is the suggestion and upon that suggestion the man throws his love. As the oyster throws over the irritants, it finds in its shell, the substance that turns the irritants into beautiful pearls, so man throws out love, and it is always man's highest ideal that he loves, and the highest ideal is always selfless; so man loves love. God is love, and we love God — or love love.

We only *see* love, love cannot be expressed. "A dumb man eating butter" cannot tell you what butter is like. Butter is butter, and its qualities cannot be expressed to those who have not tasted it. Love for love's sake cannot be expressed to those who have not felt it.

Love may be symbolised by a triangle. The first angle is, love never begs, never asks for anything; the second, love knows no fear; the third and the apex, love for love's sake. Through the power of love the senses become finer and higher. The perfect love is very rare in human relation, for human love is almost always interdependent and mutual. But God's love is a constant stream, nothing can hurt or disturb it. When man loves God as his highest ideal, as no beggar, wanting nothing, then is love carried to the extreme of evolution, and it becomes a great power in the universe. It takes a long time to get to these things, and we have to begin by that which is nearest to our nature; some are born to service, some to be mothers in love. Anyhow, the result is with God. We must take advantage of nature.

ON DOING GOOD TO THE WORLD

We are asked: What good is your Religion to society? Society is made a test of truth. Now this is very illogical. Society is only a stage of growth through which we are passing. We might just as well judge the good or utility of a scientific discovery by its use to the baby. It is simply monstrous. If the social state were permanent, it would be the same as if the baby remained a baby. There can be no perfect man-baby; the words are a contradiction in terms, so there can be no perfect society. Man must and will grow out of such early stages. Society is good at a certain stage, but it cannot be our ideal; it is a constant flux. The present mercantile civilisation must die, with all its pretensions and humbug — all a kind of "Lord Mayor's Show". What the world wants is thought-power through individuals. My Master used to say, "Why don't you help your own lotus flower to bloom? The bees will then come of themselves." The world needs people who are mad with the love of God. You must believe in yourself, and then you will believe in God. The history of the world is that of six men of faith, six men of deep pure character. We need to have three things; the heart to feel, the brain to conceive, the hand to work. First we must go out of the world and make ourselves fit instruments. Make yourself a dynamo. *Feel* first for the world. At a time when all men are ready to work, where is the man of *feeling*? Where is the feeling that produced an Ignatius Loyola? Test your love and humility. That man is not humble or loving who is jealous. Jealousy is a terrible, horrible sin; it enters a man so mysteriously. Ask yourself, does your mind react in hatred or jealousy? Good works are continually being undone by the tons of hatred and anger which are being poured out on the world. If you are pure, if you are strong, *you, one* man, are equal to the whole world.

The brain to conceive the next condition of doing good works is only a dry Sahara after all; it cannot do anything alone unless it has the *feeling* behind it. Take love, which has never failed; and then the brain will conceive, and the hand will work righteousness. Sages have dreamed of and have *seen* the vision of God. "The pure in heart shall see God." All the great ones claim to have *seen* God. Thousands of years ago has the vision been seen, and the unity which lies beyond has been recognised; and now the only thing we can do is to fill in these glorious outlines.

Mother-Worship

(Based on fragmentary notes of a class talk by Swami Vivekananda in New York.)

The two conjoint facts of perception we can never get rid of are happiness and unhappiness — things which bring us pain also bring pleasure. Our world is made up of these two. We cannot get rid of them; with every pulsation of life they are present. The world is busy trying to reconcile these opposites, sages trying to find solution of this commingling of the opposites. The burning heat of pain is intermitted by flashes of rest, the gleam of light breaking the darkness in intermittent flashes only to make the gloom deeper.

Children are born optimists, but the rest of life is a continuous disillusionment; not one ideal can be fully attained, not one thirst can be quenched. So on they go trying to solve the riddle, and religion has taken up the task.

In religions of dualism, among the Persians, there was a God and a Satan. This through the Jews has gone all over Europe and America. It was a working hypothesis thousands of years ago; but now we know, that is not tenable. There is nothing absolutely good or evil; it is good to one and evil to another, evil today, good tomorrow, and vice versa. . . .

God was first of course a clan-god, then He became God of gods. With ancient Egyptians and Babylonians, this idea (of a dual God and Satan) was very practically carried out. Their Moloch became God of gods and the captured gods were forced to do homage in His temple.

Yet the riddle remains: Who presides over this Evil? Many are hoping against hope that all is good and that we do not understand. We are clutching at a straw, burying our heads in the sand. Yet we all follow morality and the gist of morality is sacrifice — not I but thou. Yet how it clashes with the great good God of the universe! He is so selfish, the most vengeful person that we know, with plagues, famines, war!

We all have to get experiences in this life. We may try to fly bitter experiences, but sooner or later they catch us. And I pity the man who does not face the whole.

Manu Deva of the Vedas, was transformed in Persia as Ahriman. So the mythological explanation of the question was dead; but the question remained, and there was no reply, no solution.

But there was the other idea in the old Vedic hymn to the Goddess: "I am the light. I am the light of the sun and moon; I am the air which animates all beings." This is the germ which afterwards develops into Mother-worship. By Mother-worship is not meant difference between father and mother. The first idea connoted by it is that of energy — I am the power that is in all beings.

The baby is a man of nerves. He goes on and on till he is a man of power. The idea of good and evil was not at first differentiated and developed. An advancing consciousness showed power as the primal idea. Resistance and struggle at every step is the law. We are the resultant of the two — energy and resistance, internal and external power. Every atom is working and resisting every thought in the mind. Everything we see and know is but the resultant of these two forces.

This idea of God is something new. In the Vedic hymns Varuna and Indra shower the choicest gifts and blessings on devotees, a very human idea, more human than man himself.

This is the new principle. There is one power behind all phenomena. Power is power everywhere, whether in the form of evil or as Saviour of the world. So this is the new idea; the old idea was man-God. Here is the first opening out of the idea of one universal power.

"I stretch the bows of Rudra when He desires to destroy evil" (Rig-Veda, X. 125, *Devi-Sukta*).

Very soon in the Gitâ (IX. 19, also X. 4-5) we find, "O Arjuna, I am the Sat and I am the Asat, I am the good and I am the bad, I am the power of saints, I am the power of the wicked." But soon the speaker patches up truth, and the idea goes to sleep. I am power in good so long as it is doing good works.

In the religion of Persia, there was the idea of Satan, but in India, no conception of Satan. Later books began to realise this new idea. Evil exists, and there is no shirking the fact. The universe is a fact; and if a fact, it is a huge composite of good and evil. Whoever rules must rule over good and evil. If that power makes us live, the same makes us die. Laughter and tears are kin, and there are more tears than laughter in this world. Who made flowers, who made the Himalayas? — a very good God. Who made my sins and weaknesses? — Karma, Satan, self. The result is a lame, one-legged universe, and naturally the God of the universe, a one-legged God.

The view of the absolute separation of good and evil, two cut and dried and separate existences, makes us brutes of unsympathetic hearts. The good woman jumps aside from the streetwalker. Why? She may be infinitely better than you in some respects. This view brings eternal jealousy and hatred in the world, eternal barrier between man and man, between the good man and the comparatively less good or evil man. Such brutal view is pure evil, more evil than evil itself. Good and evil are not separate existences, but there is an evolution of good, and what is less good we call evil.

Some are saints and some sinners. The sun shines on good and evil alike. Does he make any distinction?

The old idea of the fatherhood of God is connected with the sweet notion of God presiding over happiness. We want to deny facts. Evil is non-existent, is zero. The "I" is evil. And the "I" exists only too much. Am I zero? Every day I try to find myself so and fail.

All these ideas are attempts to fly evil. But we have to face it. Face the whole! Am I under contract to anyone to offer partial love to God only in happiness and good, not in misery and evil ?

The lamp by the light of which one forges a name and another writes a cheque for a thousand dollars for famine, shines on both, knows no difference. Light knows no evil; you and I make it good or evil.

This idea must have a new name. It is called Mother, because in a literal sense it began long ago with a feminine writer elevated to a goddess. Then came Sânkhya, and with it all energy is female. The magnet is still, the iron filings are active.

The highest of all feminine types in India is mother, higher than wife. Wife and children may desert a man, but his mother never. Mother is the same or loves her child perhaps a little more. Mother represents colourless love that knows no barter, love that never dies. Who can have such love? — only mother, not son, nor daughter, nor wife.

"I am the Power that manifests everywhere", says the Mother — She who is bringing out this universe, and She who is bringing forth the following destruction. No need to say that destruction is only the beginning of creation. The top of a hill is only the beginning of a valley.

Be bold, face facts as facts. Do not be chased about the universe by evil. Evils are evils. What of that?

After all, it is only Mother's play. Nothing serious after all. What could move the Almighty? What made Mother create the universe? She could have no goal. Why? Because the goal is something that is not yet attained.

What is this creation for? Just fun. We forget this and begin to quarrel and endure misery. We are the playmates of the Mother.

Look at the torture the mother bears in bringing up the baby. Does she enjoy it? Surely. Fasting and praying and watching. She loves it better than anything else. Why? Because there is no selfishness.

Pleasure will come — good: who forbids? Pain will come: welcome that too. A mosquito was sitting on a bull's horn; then his conscience troubled him and he said, "Mr. Bull, I have been sitting here along time. Perhaps I annoy you. I am sorry, I will go away." But the bull replied, "Oh, no, not at all! Bring your whole family and live on my horn; what can you do to me?"

Why can we not say that to misery? To be brave is to have faith in the Mother!

"I am Life, I am Death." She it is whose shadow is life and death. She is the pleasure in all pleasure. She is the misery in all misery. If life comes, it is the Mother; if death comes, it is the Mother. If heaven comes, She is. If hell comes, there is the Mother; plunge in. We have not faith, we have not patience to see this. We trust the man in the street; but there is one being in the universe we never trust and that is God. We trust Him when He works just our way. But the time will come when, getting blow after blow, the self-sufficient mind will die. In everything we do, the serpent ego is rising up. We are glad that there are so many thorns on the path. They strike the hood of the cobra.

Last of all will come self-surrender. Then we shall be able to give ourselves up to the Mother. If misery comes, welcome; if happiness comes, welcome. Then, when we come up to this love, all crooked things shall be straight. There will be the same sight for the Brahmin, the Pariah, and the dog. Until we love the universe with same-sightedness, with impartial, undying love, we are missing again and again. But then all will have vanished, and we shall see in all the same infinite eternal Mother.

Narada-Bhakti-Sutras

(A free translation dictated by Swamiji in America)

CHAPTER I

1. Bhakti is intense love for God.

2. It is the nectar of love;

3. Getting which man becomes perfect, immortal, and satisfied for ever;

4. Getting which man desires no more, does not become jealous of anything, does not take pleasure in vanities:

5. Knowing which man becomes filled with spirituality, becomes calm, and finds pleasure only in God.

6. It cannot be used to fill any desire, itself being the check to all desires.

7. Sannyâsa is giving up both the popular and the scriptural forms of worship.

8. The Bhakti-Sannyasin is the one whose whole soul goes unto God, and whatever militates against love to God, he rejects.

9. Giving up all other refuge, he takes refuge in God.

10. Scriptures are to be followed as long as one's life has not become firm;

11. Or else there is danger of doing evil in the name of liberty.

12. When love becomes established, even social forms are given up, except those which are necessary for the preservation of life.

13. There have been many definitions of love, but Nârada gives these as the signs of love: When all thoughts, all words, and all deeds are given up unto the Lord, and the least forgetfulness of God makes one intensely miserable, then *love has begun.*

14. As the Gopis had it —

15. Because, although worshipping God as their lover, they never forgot his God-nature;

16. Otherwise they would have committed the sin of unchastity.

17. This is the highest form of love, because there is no desire of reciprocity, which desire is in all human love.

CHAPTER II

1. Bhakti is greater than Karma, greater than Jnâna, greater than Yoga (Râja-Yoga), because Bhakti itself is its result, because Bhakti is both the means and the end (fruit).

2. As a man cannot satisfy his hunger by simple knowledge or sight of food, so a man cannot be satisfied by the knowledge or even the perception of God until love comes; therefore love is the highest.

CHAPTER III

1. These, however, the Masters have said about Bhakti:

2. One who wants this Bhakti must give up sense enjoyments and even the company of people.

3. Day and night he must think about Bhakti and nothing else.

4. (He must) go where they sing or talk of God.

5. The principal cause of Bhakti is the mercy of a great (or free) soul.

6. Meeting with a great soul is hard to obtain, and never fails to save the soul.

7. Through the mercy of God we get such Gurus.

8. There is no difference between Him and His (own) ones.

9. Seek, therefore, for this.

10. Evil company is always to be shunned;

11. Because it leads to lust and anger, illusion, forgetfulness of the goal, destruction of the will (lack of perseverance), and destruction of everything.

12. These disturbances may at first be like ripples, but evil company at last makes them like the sea.

13. He gets across Maya who gives up all attachment, serves the great ones, lives alone, cuts the bandages of this world, goes beyond the qualities of nature, and depends upon the Lord for even his living.

14. He who gives up the fruits of work, he who gives up all work and the dualism of joy and misery, who gives up even the scriptures, gets that unbroken love for God;

15. He crosses this river and helps others to cross it.

CHAPTER IV

1. The nature of love is inexpressible.

2. As the dumb man cannot express what he tastes, but his actions betray his feelings, so man cannot express this love in words, but his actions betray it.

3. In some rare persons it is expressed.

4. Beyond all qualities, all desires, ever increasing, unbroken, the finest perception is love.

5. When a men gets this love, he sees love everywhere he hears love everywhere, he talks love everywhere, he thinks love everywhere.

6. According to the qualities or conditions, this love manifests itself differently.

7. The qualities are: Tamas (dullness, heaviness), Rajas (restlessness, activity), Sattva (serenity, purity); and the conditions are: Ârta (afflicted), Arthârthi (wanting something), Jijnâsu (searching truth), Jnâni, (knower).

8. Of these the latter are higher than the preceding ones.

9. Bhakti is the easiest way of worship.

10. It is its own proof and does not require any other.

11. Its nature is peace and perfect bliss.

12. Bhakti never seeks to injure anyone or anything not even the popular modes of worship.

13. Conversation about lust, or doubt of God or about one's enemies must not be listened to.

14. Egotism, pride, etc. must be given up.

15. If those passions cannot be controlled, place them upon God, and place all your actions on Him.

16. Merging the trinity of Love, Lover, and Beloved, worship God as His eternal servant, His eternal bride — thus love is to be made unto God.

CHAPTER V

1. That love is highest which is concentrated upon God.

2. When such speak of God, their voices stick in their throats, they cry and weep; and it is they who give holy places their holiness; they make good works, good books better, because they are permeated with God.

3. When a man loves God so much, his forefathers rejoice, the gods dance, and the earth gets a Master!

4. To such lovers there is no difference of caste, sex, knowledge, form, birth, or wealth;

5. Because they are all God's.

6. Arguments are to be avoided;

7. Because there is no end to them, and they lead to no satisfactory result.

8. Read books treating of this love, and do deeds which increase it.

9. Giving up all desires of pleasure and pain, gain and loss, worship God day and night. Not a moment is to be spent in vain.

10. Ahimsâ (non-killing), truthfulness, purity, mercy, and godliness are always to be kept.

11. Giving up all other thoughts, the whole mind should day and night worship God. Thus being worshipped day and night, He reveals Himself and makes His worshippers feel Him.

12. In past, present, and future, *Love is greatest*!

Thus following the ancient sages, we have dared to preach the doctrine of *Love*, without fearing the jeers of the world.

biochemical mechanisms, 135–174
genetic basis, 121–134
Reverse transcriptase
inhibition by nucleoside analogs, 73–75
inhibition by non-nucleosides, 75
mutations in, 166
Ribavirin
antiviral effects, 70–71
enhancement of host immunity by, 71–72
inhibition of IMP dehydrogenase, 71
inhibition of viral capping, 71
structure, 71
Ribosome
cycle, 88
protection and tetracycline resistance, 170–171
proteins, 85
RNA, 85
role in peptide bond synthesis, 86
target for for antibiotics, 85
types, 85–86
structure, 85–87
subunits, 85–86
X-ray analysis of structure, 86–87
Rifampicin
clinical use, 79
inhibition of bacterial RNA polymerase, 79–80
resistance to, 164
structure, 110
Rifampin *see* rifampicin
Rifamycins *see* rifampicin
Ritonavir
induction of insulin resistance in patients, 110
inhibition of HIV protease, 109–110
in combination therapy for AIDS, 109
resistance to, 166–167
structure, 110
RNA biosynthesis
effects of inhibition on protein biosynthesis, 65
inhibition by rifamycins, 79–80
inhibition by streptolydigin, 80
inhibition by streptovaricins, 80
RNA polymerase
inhibition by antibiotics, 79–80
subunit structure, 80
R-plasmids
classification, 145
mechanism of transfer, 144–145
relationship to F-factors, 145
role in spread of drug-resistance, 145
structure, 142–143

Salvarsan
efficacy against syphilis, 4, 5
metabolism to mapharsen, 6
structure, 4
Saquinavir, 110
SARS, *see* Severe Acute Respiratory Syndrome
Severe Acute Respiratory Syndrome, 2
Screening
in drug discovery, 5, 114
high-throughput, 14
Paul Ehrlich, 5
targeted, 14–15
Sedimentation coefficient of DNA, effect of intercalating dyes, 81
Selectivity in antimicrobial action, 13
Semmelweiss, Ignaz, 3
Septum formation, effect of β-lactam antibiotics, 37
Sex pili role in bacterial conjugation, 144
Sleeping sickness
atoxyl treatment, 4
eflornithine treatment, 119
melarsoprol treatment, 118
see also Trypanosomiasis
Spectinomycin
biochemical action, 96
structure, 95
Sterilants, 47
Sterol biosynthesis inhibition
by allylamines, 63
by azoles, 61–63
by morpholines, 63–64
Sterols in fungal membrane, binding of polyene antibiotics, 60–61
Streptogramins
inhibition of protein biosynthesis, 102
resistance to, 160–161
synergism between Types A and B, 101–102
Streptolydigin, inhibitor of bacterial RNA polymerase, 80
Streptomycin
adenylylation of, 159–160
antibacterial action, 92–94
binding to ribosomes, 93–94
clinical use, 92
discovery, 8
effects on protein biosynthesis, 92–93
induction of codon misreading, 93–94
mode of entry into bacterial cells, 132–133
phosphorylation, 159–160
possible inhibition of *trans*-translation of messenger RNA, 96
resistance, 159–160
structure, 92
toxicity, 92
Streptovaricins
inhibitors of bacterial RNA polymerase, 80
structure, 79
Sulfazecin, 35, 36
Sulfamethoxazole, combination with trimethoprim, 69
Sulfanilamide
biochemical action, 67
metabolic product from Prontosil rubrum, 66
structure, 66
Sulfonamides
antibacterial activity, 66
competition with *p*-aminobenzoate, 67
inhibition of synthesis of dihydropteroic acid, 67
resistance to, 165
Suramin
inhibition of trypanosomal enzymes, 117
structure, 7
uptake into trypanosomes, 117
Syphilis treatment by salvarsan, 5

Teichoic acid
labile linkage to peptidoglycan, 18, 28–29
possible function, 18
possible influence on drug penetration, 18
structure, 18, 28
Teichoplanin
inhibitor of bacterial cell wall biosynthesis, 32–33
structure, 32
Teichuronic acid, 18
Telithromycin
inhibitor of protein biosynthesis, 100–101
structure, 101
Tenofovir
antiviral drug, 73–74
inhibitor of reverse transcriptase, 74–75
structure, 73
Terbinafine
antifungal use, 63
inhibition of squalene epoxidation in fungi, 63
structure, 64
Termination in protein biosynthesis, 90
Terminator codons, 90
Tetracyclines
active uptake by bacterial cells, 131
antimicrobial actions, 96
binding to ribosomes, 97
chelating activity, 97
efflux of, 131
inhibition of aminoacyl tRNA-ribosome interaction, 96–97
mechanisms of resistance to, 167–169, 171–171
ribosomal site of action, 97
selectivity of antibacterial action, 96
structure-activity relationships, 96–98
structures, 97, 99
Tetrahydrofolate
biosynthesis, 67
double blockage of synthesis, 69
importance in nucleotide synthesis, 69–70

Index

Thienamycin
  antibacterial action, 36
  resistance to β-lactamase, 36
  structure, 35
Thiol groups possible involvement in antimicrobial action of arsenicals, 118
Thymidine kinase
  activation of acyclovir, 72
  activation of azidothymidine, 73–74
Thymidylate synthase, inhibition by 5-fluorodeoxyuridine, 70
Ticarcillin, 34, 35
Tigicycline
  action against tetracycline-resistant bacteria, 168
  structure, 99
Tolnaftate
  clinical use, 63
  inhibition of squalene epoxidation, 63
  structure, 64
Topoisomerases
  functions of, 75–76
  DNA gyrase, 76
  inhibitors, 76–79
  supercoiling of DNA, 75–76
  types of, 76
Toxophore, 5
Transduction
  generalized, 146
  possible contribution to spread of drug-resistance, 146
  specialized, 146
Transfer RNA
  binding to ribosomes, 89
  conversion to aminoacyl transfer (t) RNA, 87
  translocation in protein biosynthesis, 89
Transformation
  contribution to the spread of drug-resistance, 147
  mechanism of, 146–147
Transglycolase
  component of penicillin-binding proteins, 27
  inhibition by vancomycin, 33
  role in peptidoglycan biosynthesis, 24
Translational domain on ribosomes, 86
Translocation
  inhibition by cycloheximide, 104
  inhibition by fusidic acid, 103
  in protein biosynthesis, 89
Transpeptidase
  inhibition by β-lactams, 37–39
  in peptidoglycan cross-linking, 27
Transposons
  in drug-resistance, 140–142
  insertion mechanism, 140, 141, 142
  structure, 141
  see also Conjugative transposons
Triclosan
  antiseptic, 50
  inhibitor of fatty acid biosynthesis, 51–52
  structure, 49
Tridemorph, 64
Trimethoprim
  resistance, 164–165
  selective inhibition of bacterial dihydrofolate reductase, 69
  structure, 68
Trypan red, antitrypanosomal action 4
Trypanosomes
  kinetoplast DNA and intercalating molecules, 83
  glycolysis in, 117, 118
  polyamines synthesis in, 119
  redox balance in, 118
Trypanosomiasis
  current treatments, 117–119
  forms of, 117
Trypanothione
  role in redox control in trypanosomes, 118
  interaction with melarsoprol, 117
Tuberculosis
  resurgence of, 1
  treatment with synthetic compounds, 39–41
  treatment with antibiotics, 79, 92
Tyrocidin A
  action on membranes, 52, 53
  structure, 52

UDP-*N*-acetylmuramic acid biosynthesis, 22
Undecaprenyl phosphate in peptidoglycan biosynthesis, 24
Undecaprenyl pyrophosphatase, 24
Uptake of antimicrobial drugs, 129–133
Uridine nucleotides of *N*-acetyl muramic acid
  accumulation caused by inhibitors of peptidoglycan biosynthesis, 30
  biosynthesis, 22

Valinomycin
  mechanism of potassium complex formation, 54–56
  mobile carrier of ions, 54–56
  structure, 55
Vancomycin
  antibacterial activity, 32
  binding to D-alanyl-D-alanine group, 32–33
  dimerization, 33
  inhibition of transglycolase, 33
  resistance, 71–72
  structure, 32
Variable surface glycoprotein in trypanosomes, 119
Vidarabine *see* Arabinosyl adenine
Virus infections, chemotherapy of, 70–75 109–113
Voriconazole
  antifungal spectrum, 62
  structure, 63

Waksman, Selman, 8
West Nile fever, 2

Zanamavir
  action against influenza, 111–112
  inhibitor of viral neuraminidsase, 112
  structure, 112